TO ABSTRACT:

Sarah Miller and Jack Doehring

East/West Publishing

Front Cover:
Sarah Miller
'Open #71'
mixed media on slate, 2013

For print inquiries of Sarah Miller's 'Open' series, please visit www.aclew.org

ISBN: 978-0615911670
LCCN: 2013954684

For our ancestors, especially the creative ones

CONTENTS

Introduction

What interests me about Sarah Miller's artwork is her depiction of space as well as her ability to match concept with style and material. The images in this book evoke the expansiveness of space and the vast potential of the human mind. The chalk, slate and water Sarah Miller uses are basic materials, however, the diverse and animated images she creates demonstrates how creativity can approach the infinite. The chalk and slate also reference the classroom, teaching, learning and language which add an educational dimension to her 'Open' series. Miller's fluid calligraphy like marks foster the formation of thoughts which encourages deep thinking. Sarah Miller's artwork is constantly balancing the world of form and formlessness.

The poetry in this book is a personal response to Sarah Miller's art. To begin, my process involves the free-writing of thoughts, emotions, words, concepts and narrative. The myriad of associations which enter the mind after contemplating Sarah Miller's work inspires my poems. After compiling my reactions, the next step is to seek patterns or associations which form a theme or story. From there, the composition takes shape after speaking the poems out loud to determine the rhythm or placement of certain words. My goal for a completed poem is not only to have a concept, but also a temporal narrative to create a beginning, a body and an end. I use vivid, yet concise words often without prepositions, conjunctions or pronouns. This method keeps the poems fresh, rhythmic and abstract as a compliment to the visual art.

Jack Doehring

To Abstract

To abstract comes from the Latin language, to take from is the literal translation. To abstract is to break down in to elemental form, to simplify. If we look at the work of Henri Matisse, the modern master, he elegantly used elemental line to describe the human face. To translate the human figure well, to render the figure artfully with few lines requires great skill and sensitivity to the entire surface and materials because the artist cuts away the unnecessary to arrive at the essence of the subject. The same can be said for pure abstraction or non-objective painting and drawing. In non-objective art, there is no reference to the outside world rather the artist employs the art elements (line, shape, form, space, value, texture and color) driven by an internal subject matter. In the contemporary age, multimedia is often used to create artworks which are innovated. It is more difficult to invent than it is to merely copy from the outside world. The viewer can ponder the world of abstraction through the impact of emotion similar to the way in which people appreciate music. When a person listens to a guitar solo with no lyrics, the same impact can be felt through pure abstraction, however, the viewer must open the mind. Abstract art should communicate a human experience.

The Void

In the Eastern conception of space, there is a synthesis of the whole composition rather than in the over taught Western conception of space, originating from the Renaissance. In my professional work, I employ an Eastern conception of space. If the viewer considers the void as a galaxy, a great empty space which becomes animated through the marks created by the artist – an entirely new perspective opens. There is no foreground or background rather all the elements in the composition are equal players. The void requires little to become activated thus 'empty' space becomes crucial to the overall composition. The art elements come together to create a symphony of balance.

'Open' series, 2013

To Abstract: features my multimedia 'Open' series in chalk, pastel and water on slate employing an improvisational drawing process which is photographed to document a specific state or perspective. The artworks are intentionally non-permanent like the transitory nature of life. The photographic prints are 'untouched' or not altered digitally to maintain subtle imperfections and textures. Through the freestyle poems of Jack Doehring, the viewer is given a window in a literary sense to appreciate pure abstraction via the universal.

Sarah Miller

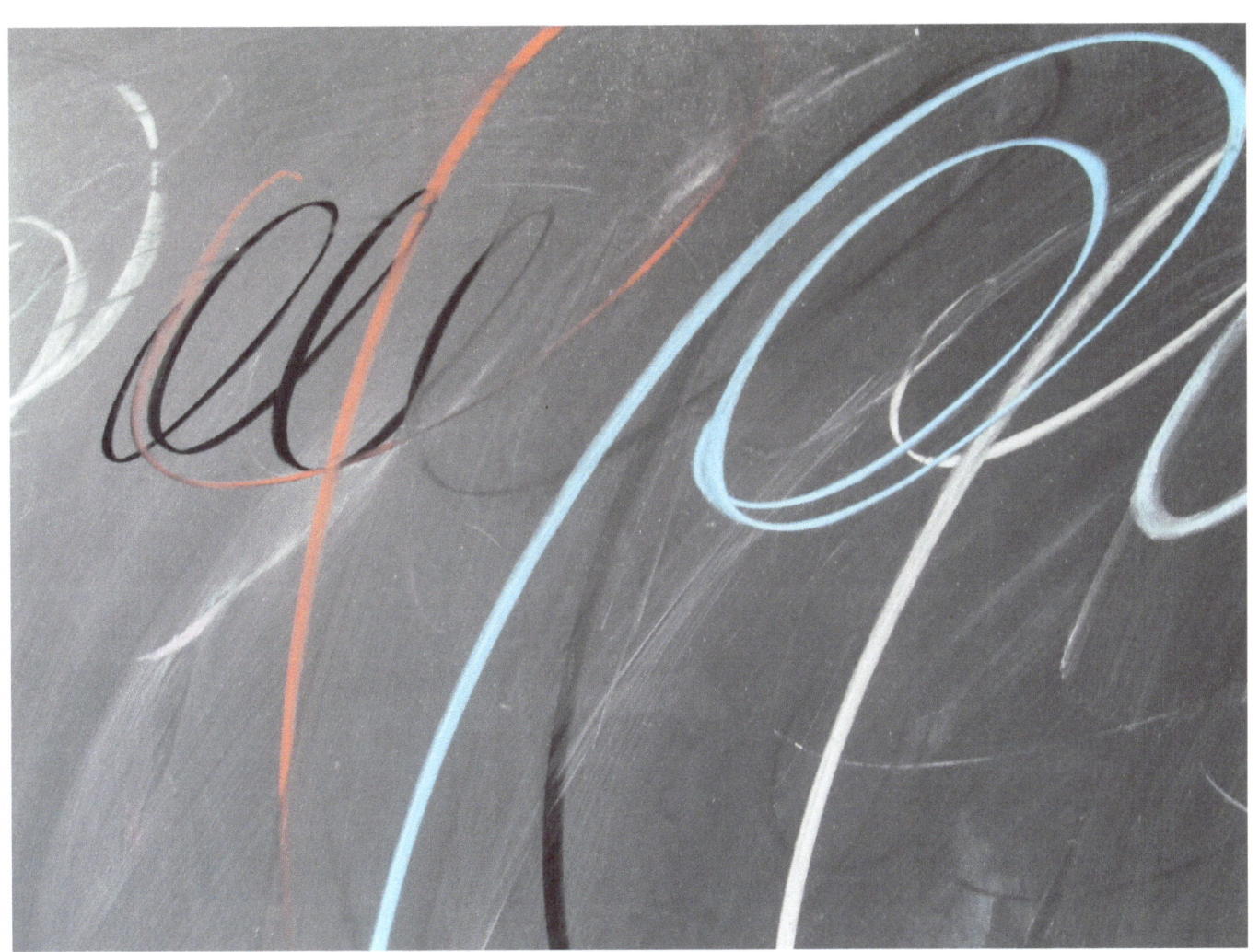

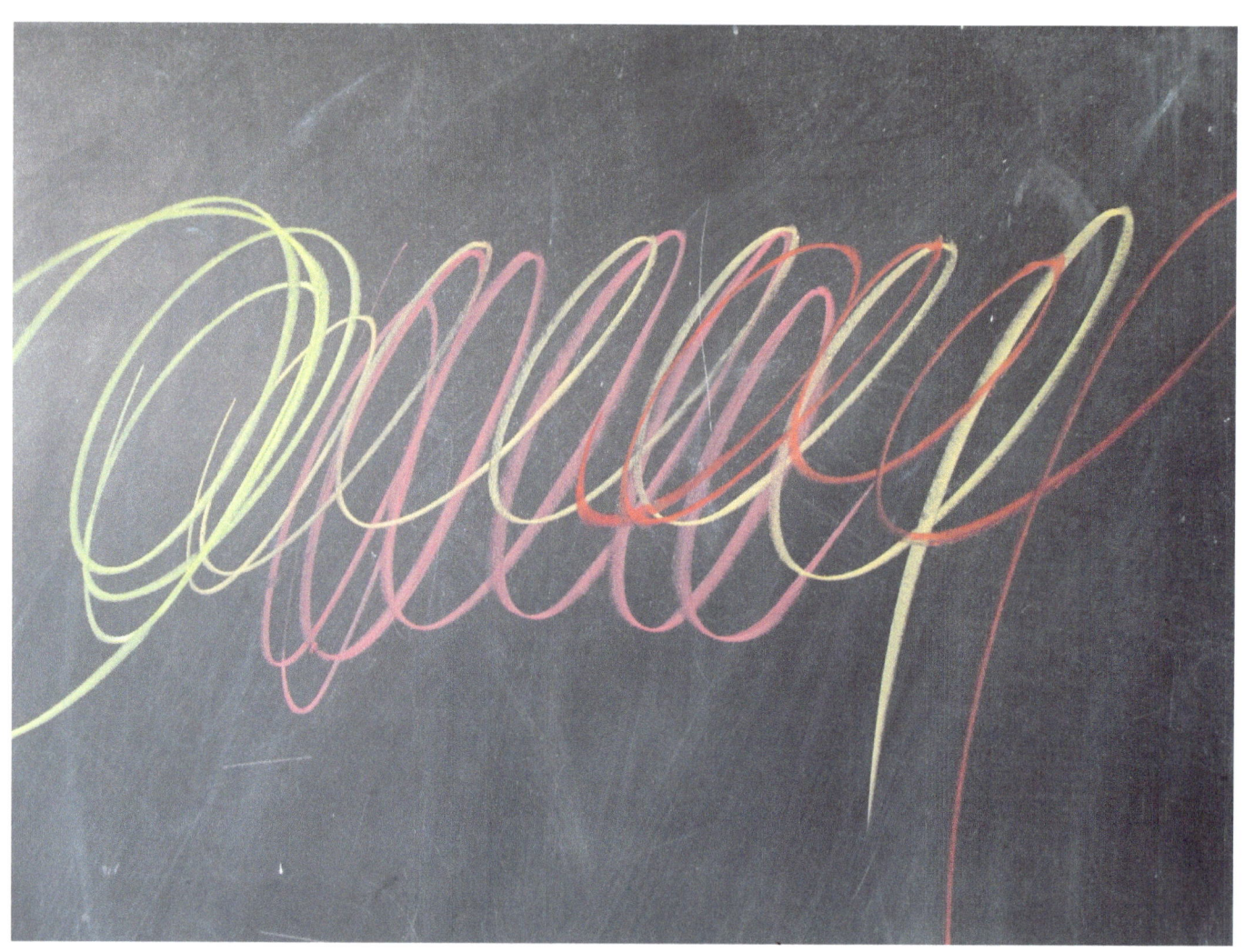

faces disappear
golden moon
broken taijitu
tranquil light

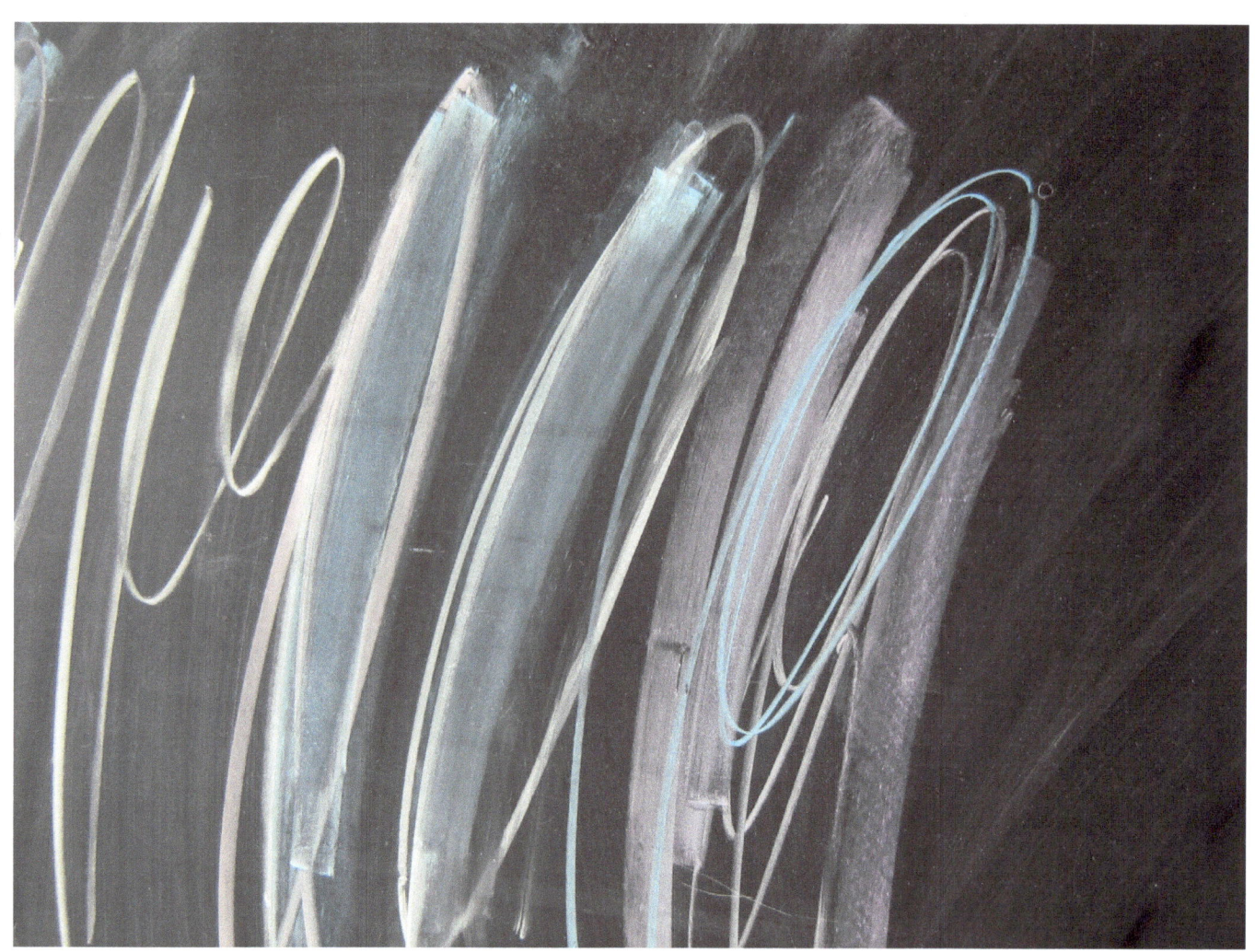

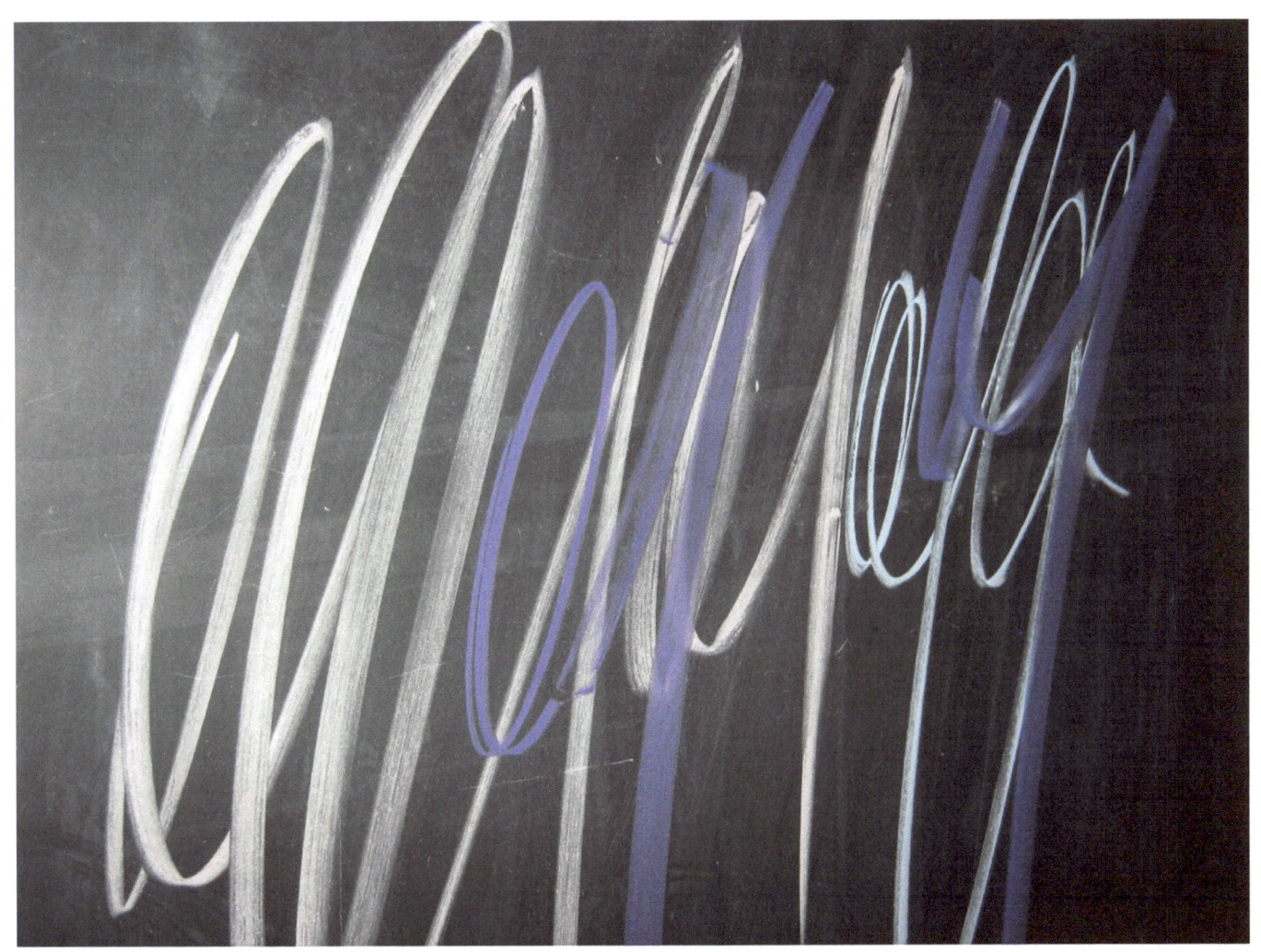

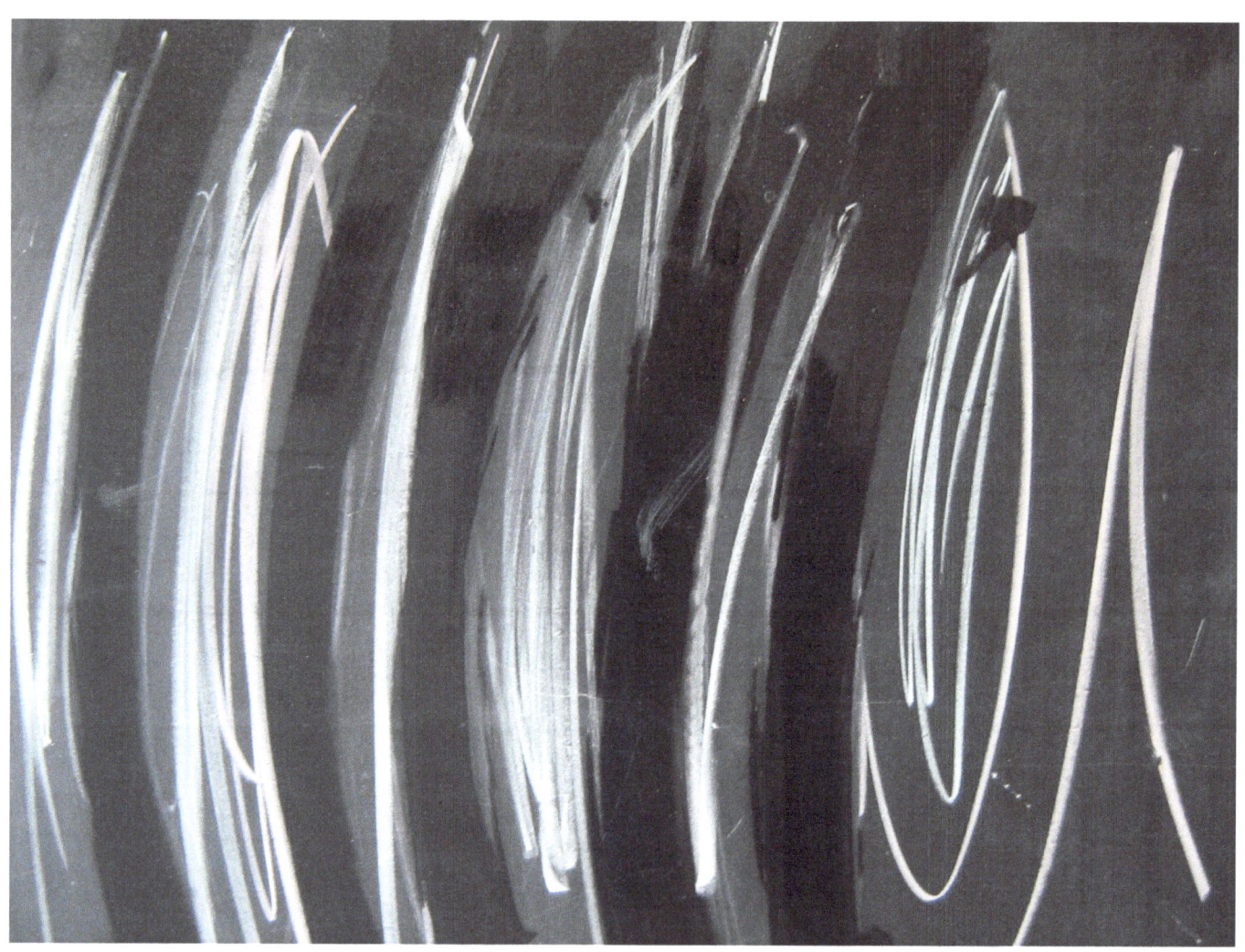

horizon melting
glaciers speaking
crashing cliffs
we don't hear

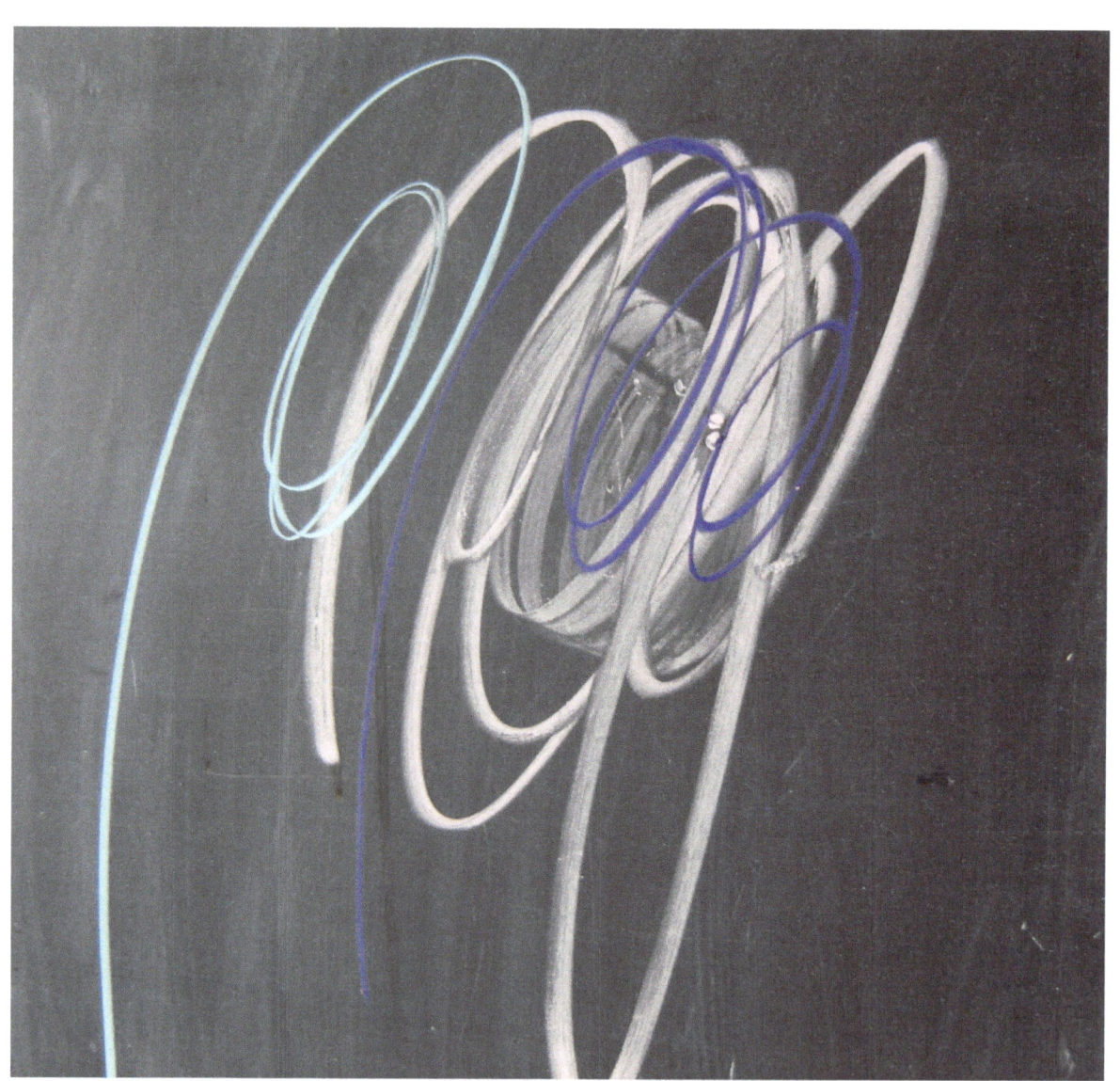

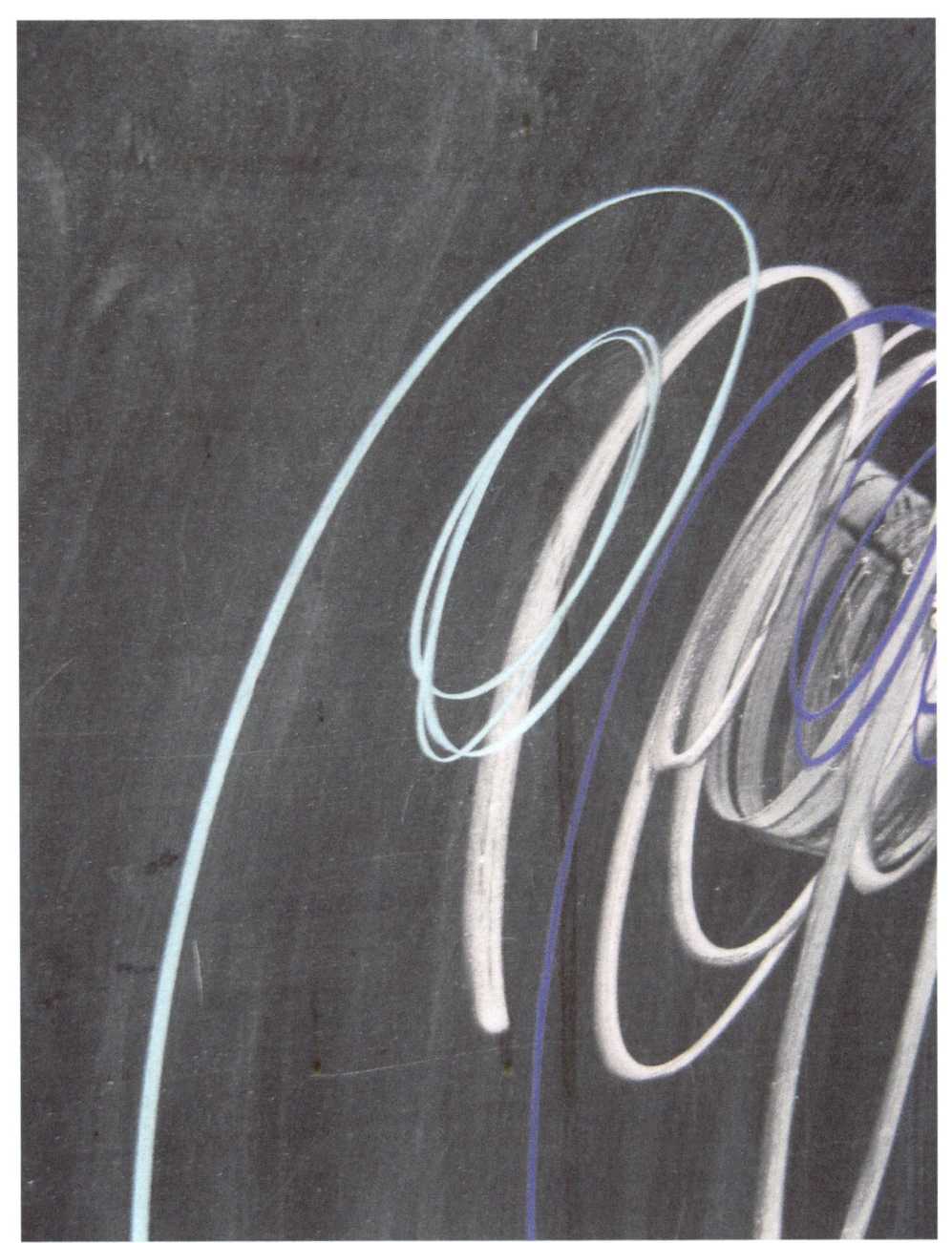

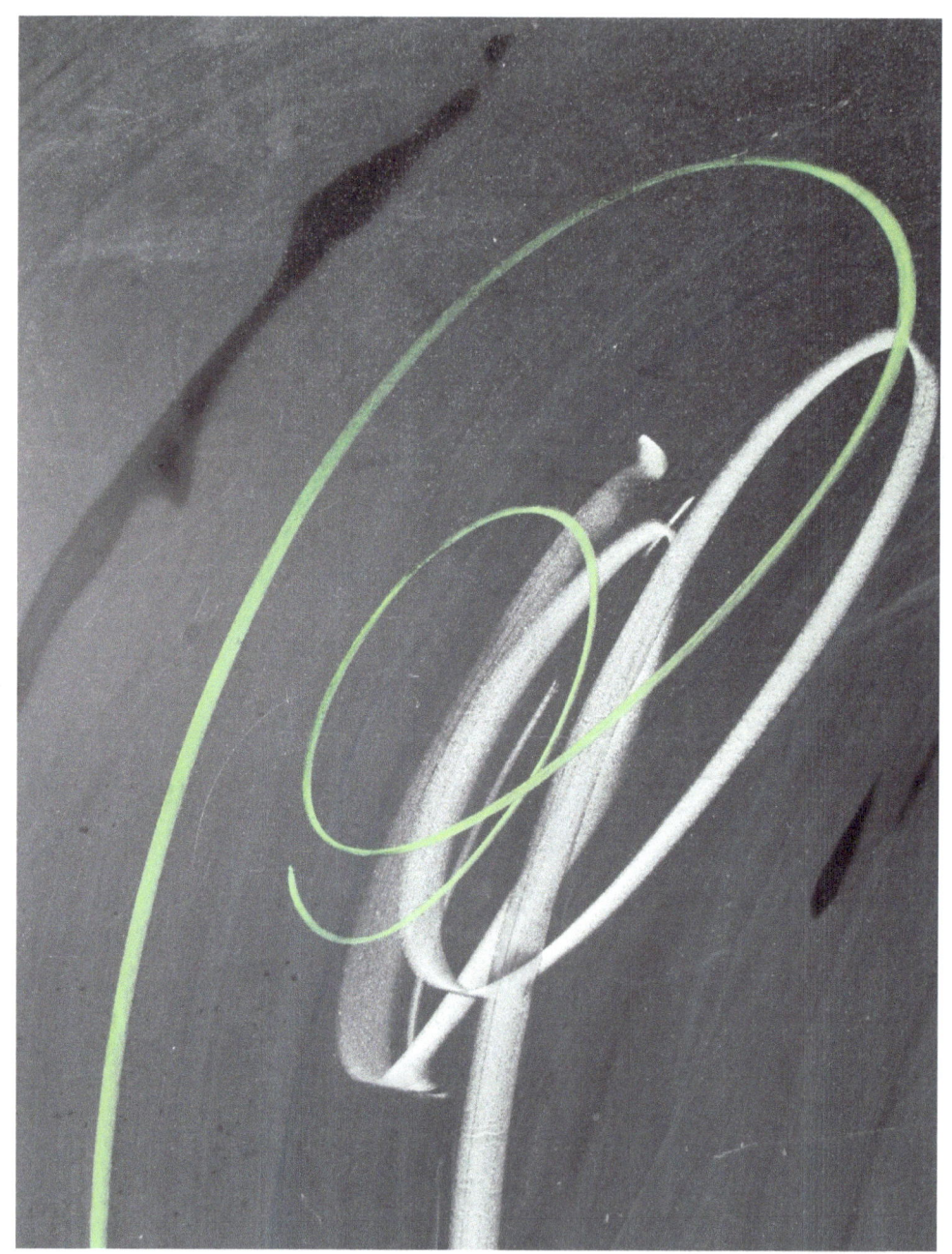

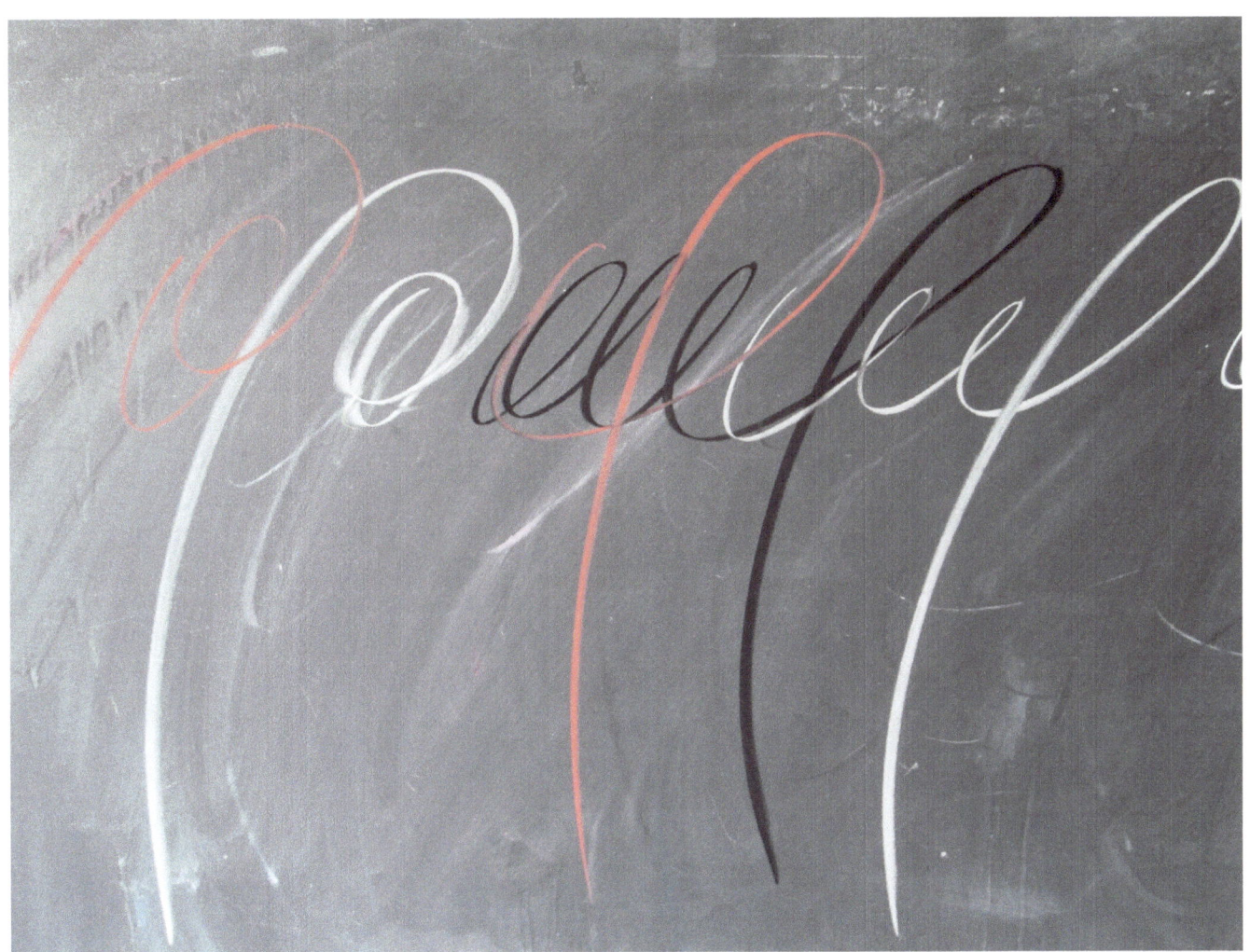

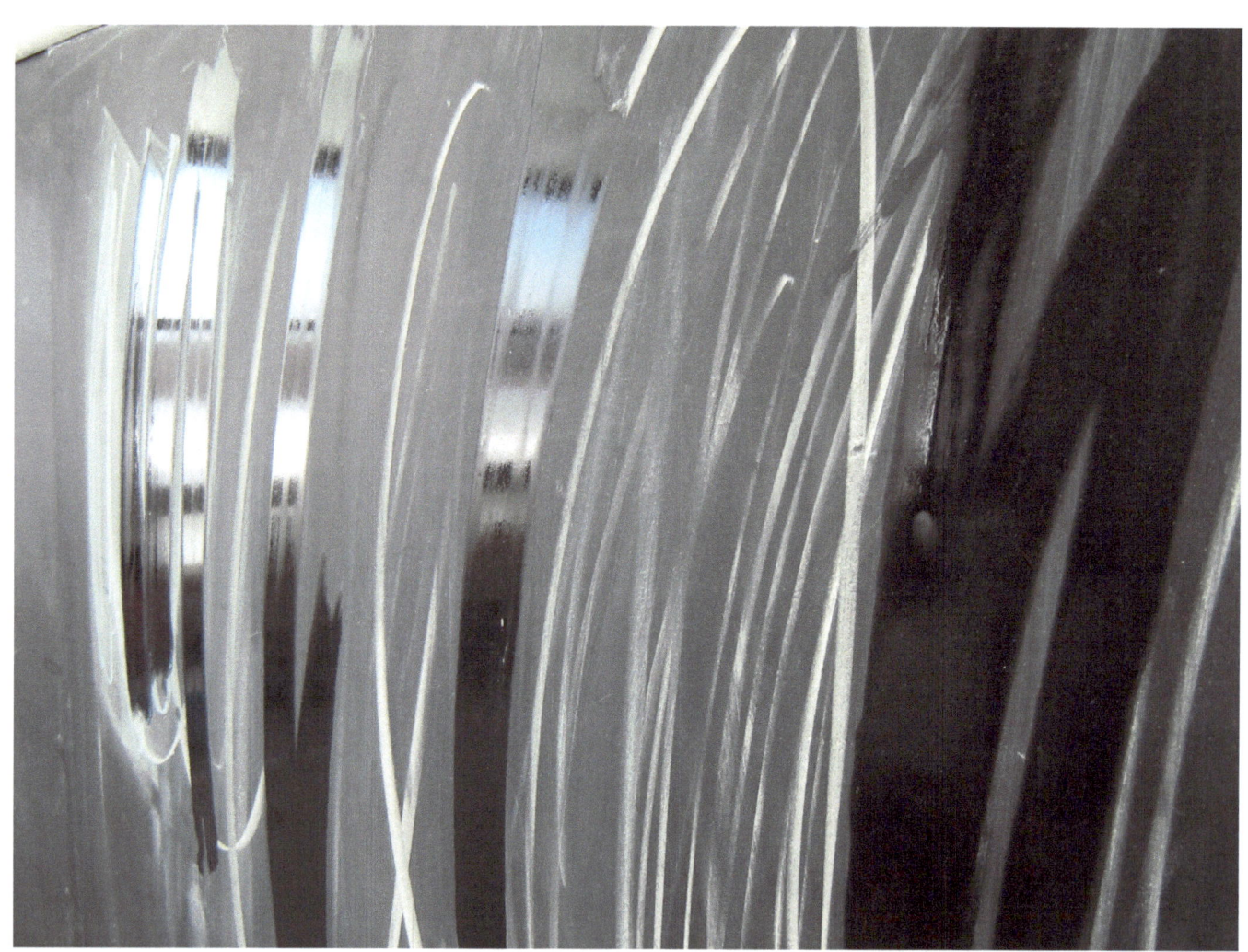

girl walking darkness
memories raw silent
reflecting empty scars
waves forever howling
skies echo heal

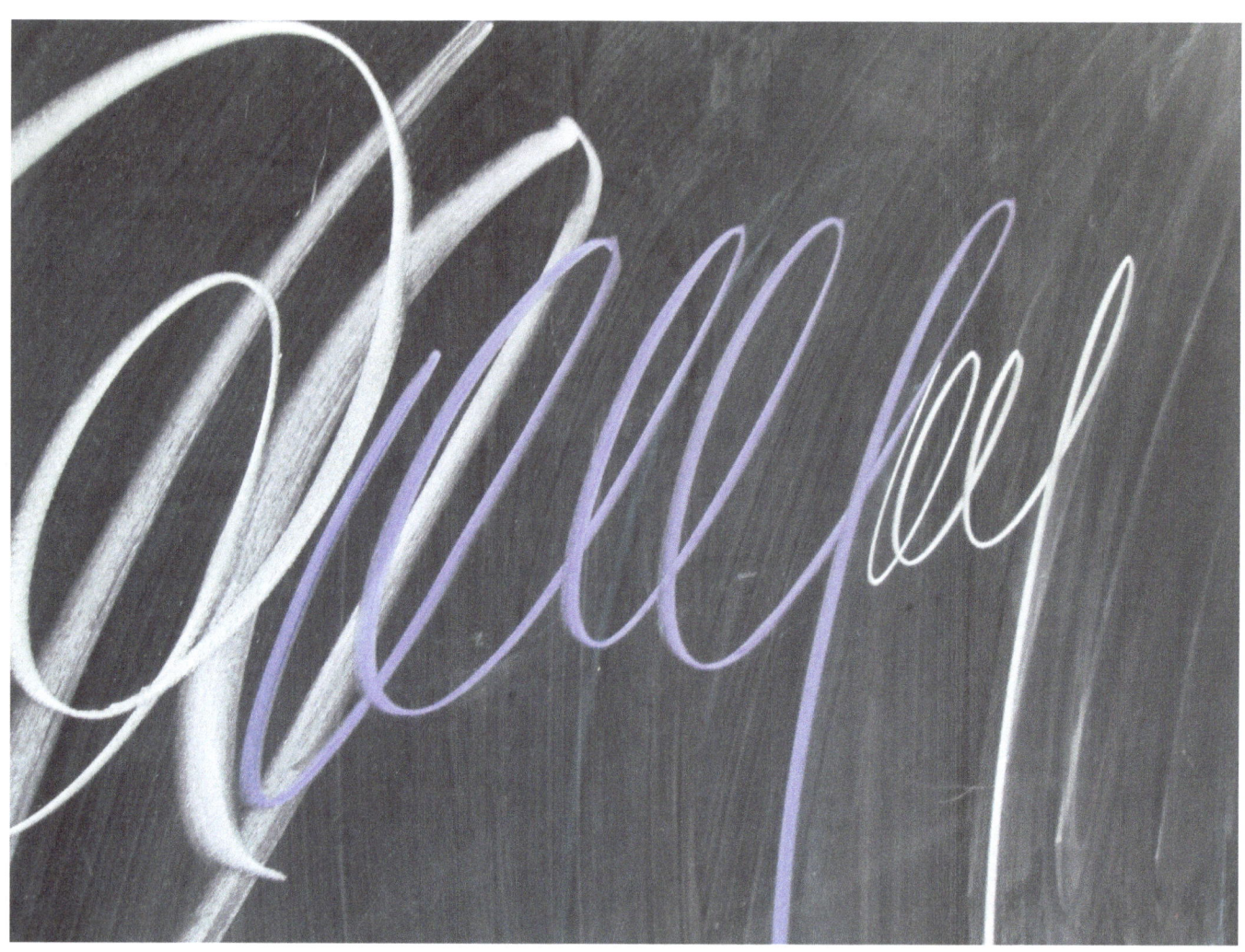

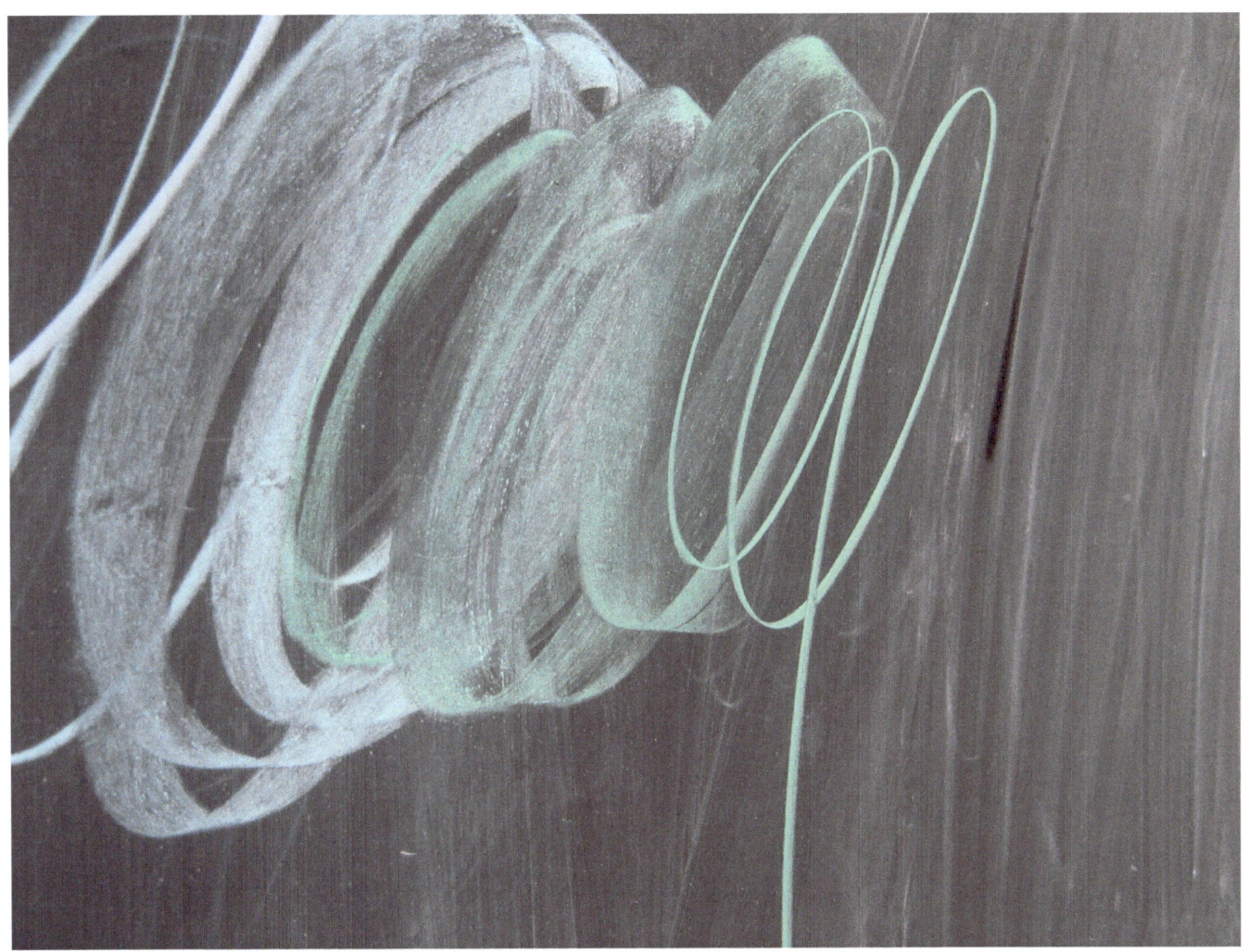

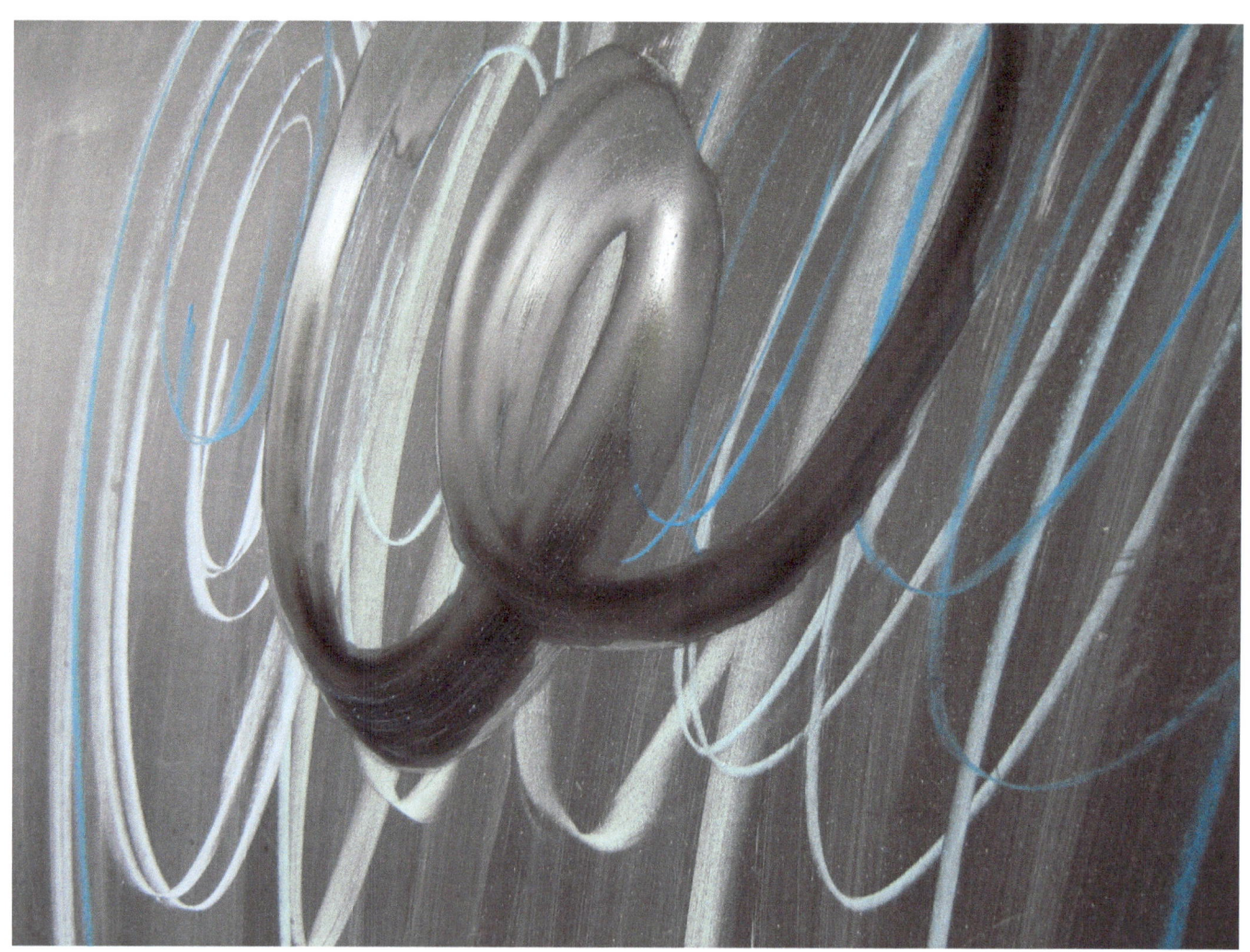

painted portrait
eyes like jewels
lips like the sun
neck like a crescent moon

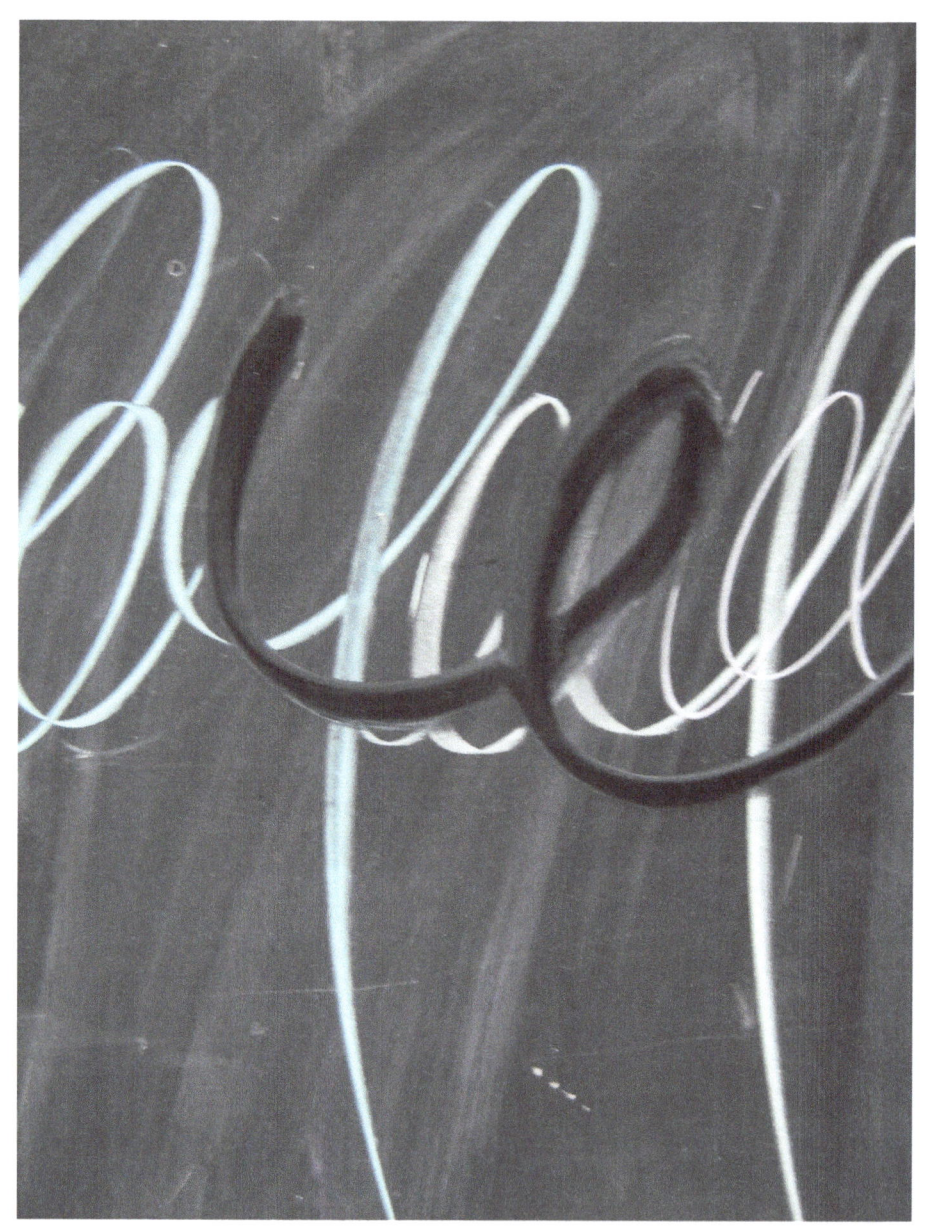

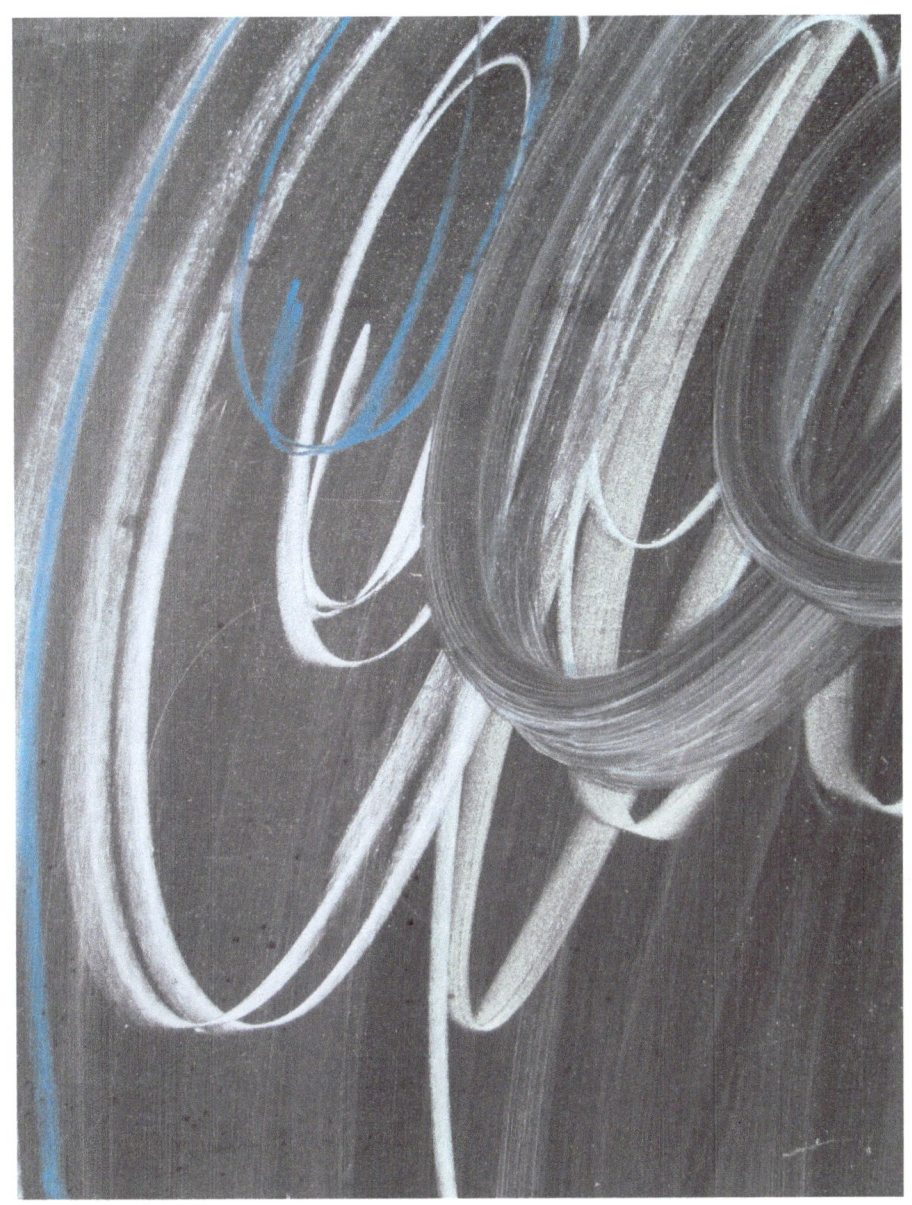

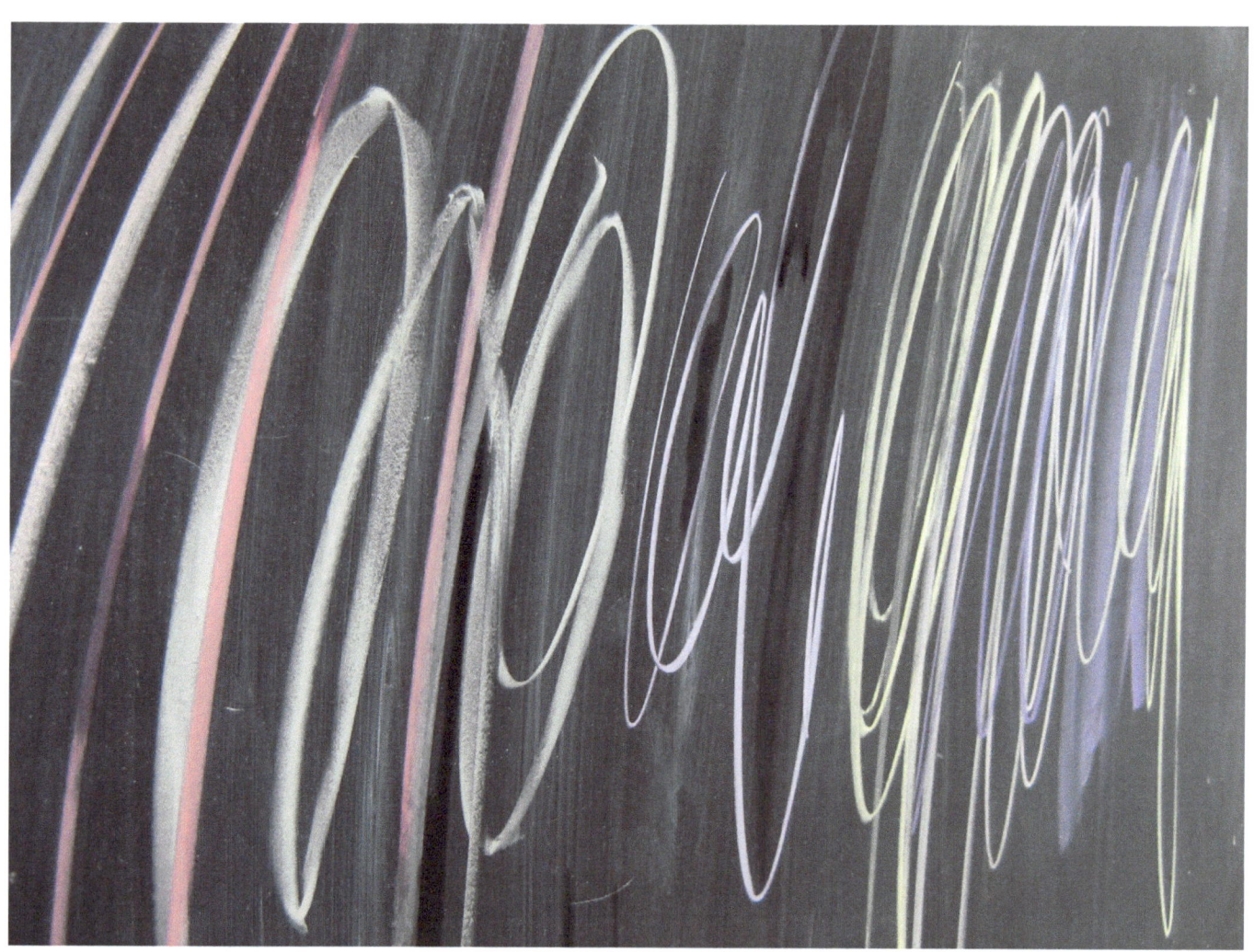

sunflowers pray
grooms vow
dresses billow
the chapel listens

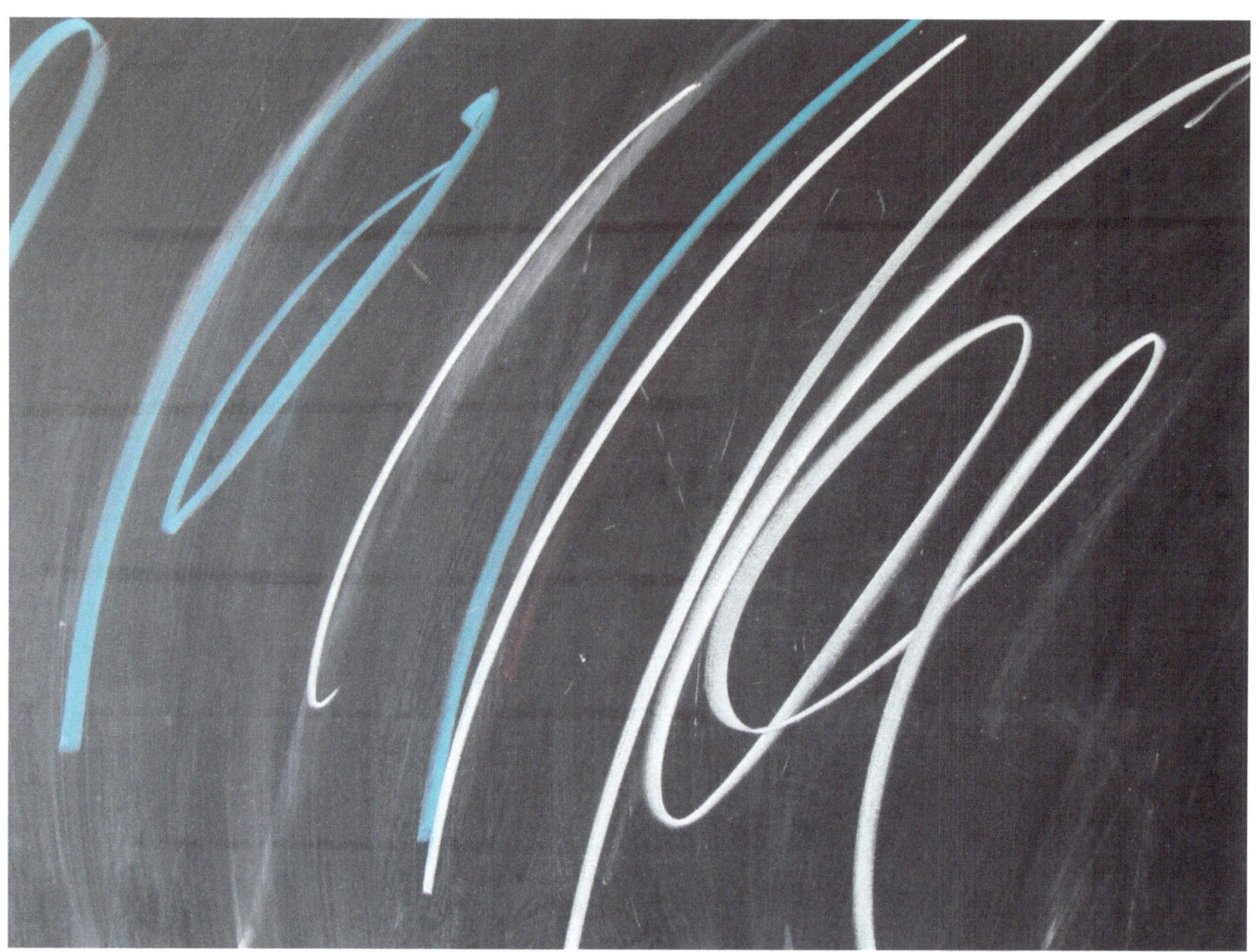

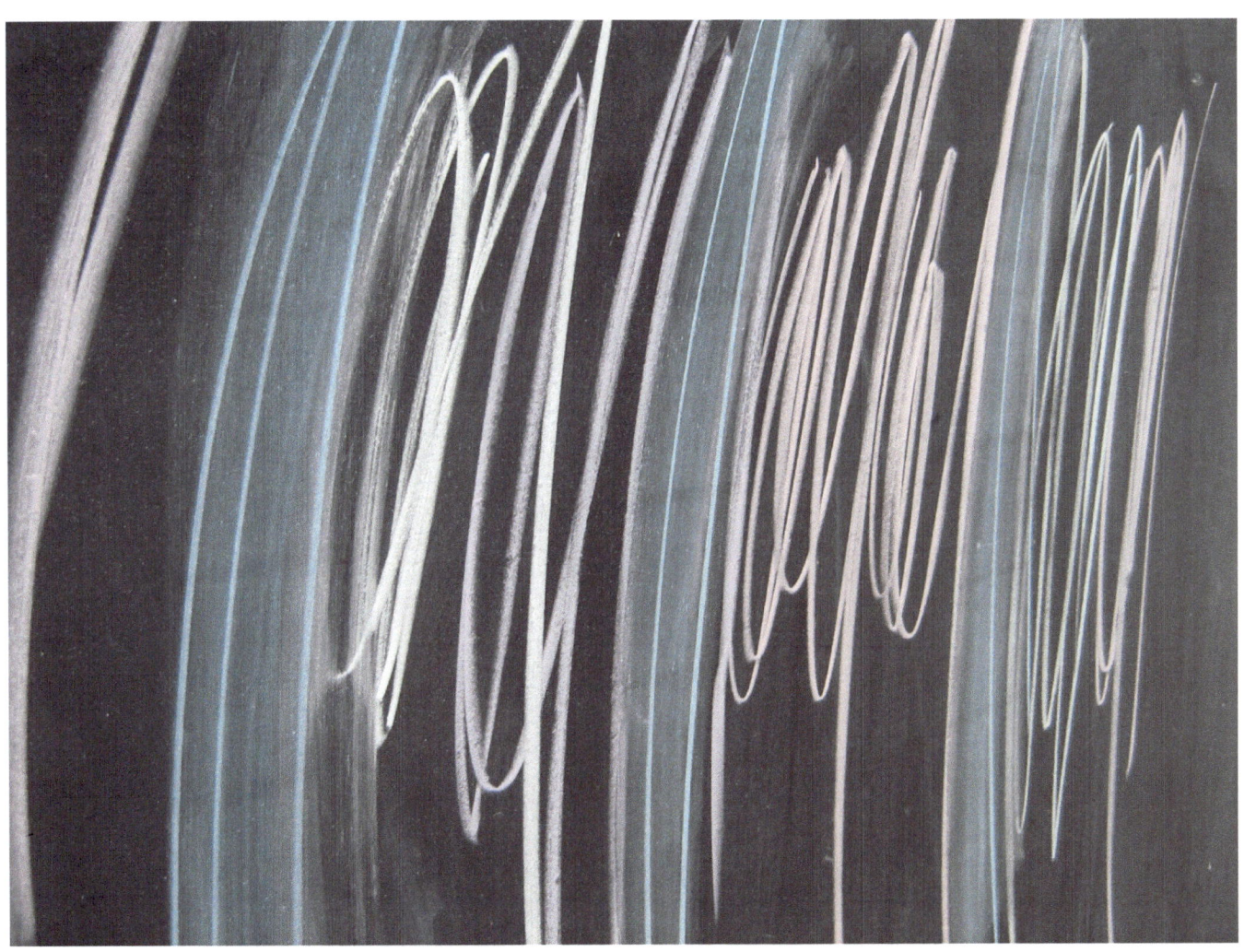

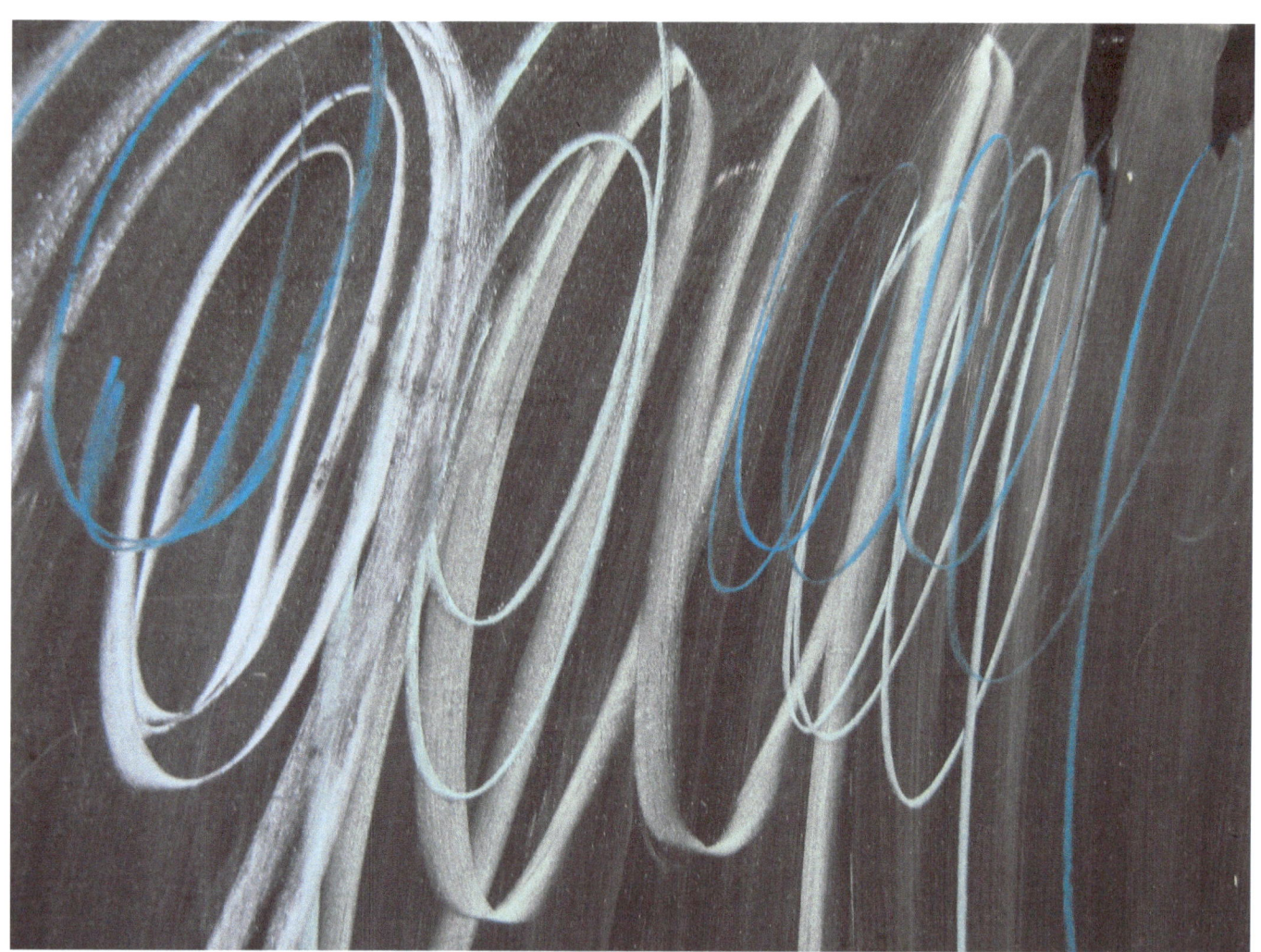

young man wandering
empty tattered jeans

lost man
mind unraveled

I am unable to speak
words have no power
with the face of insanity

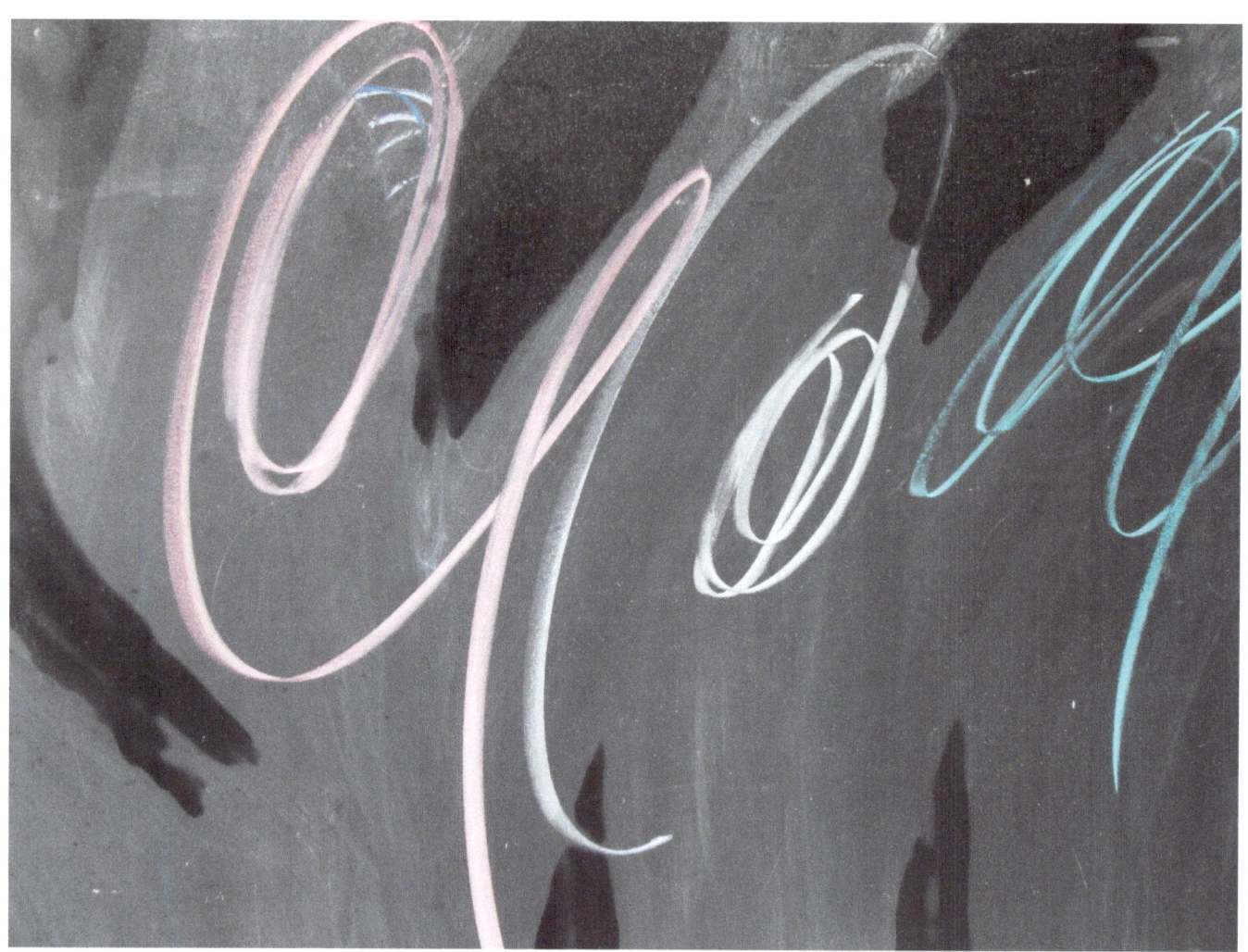

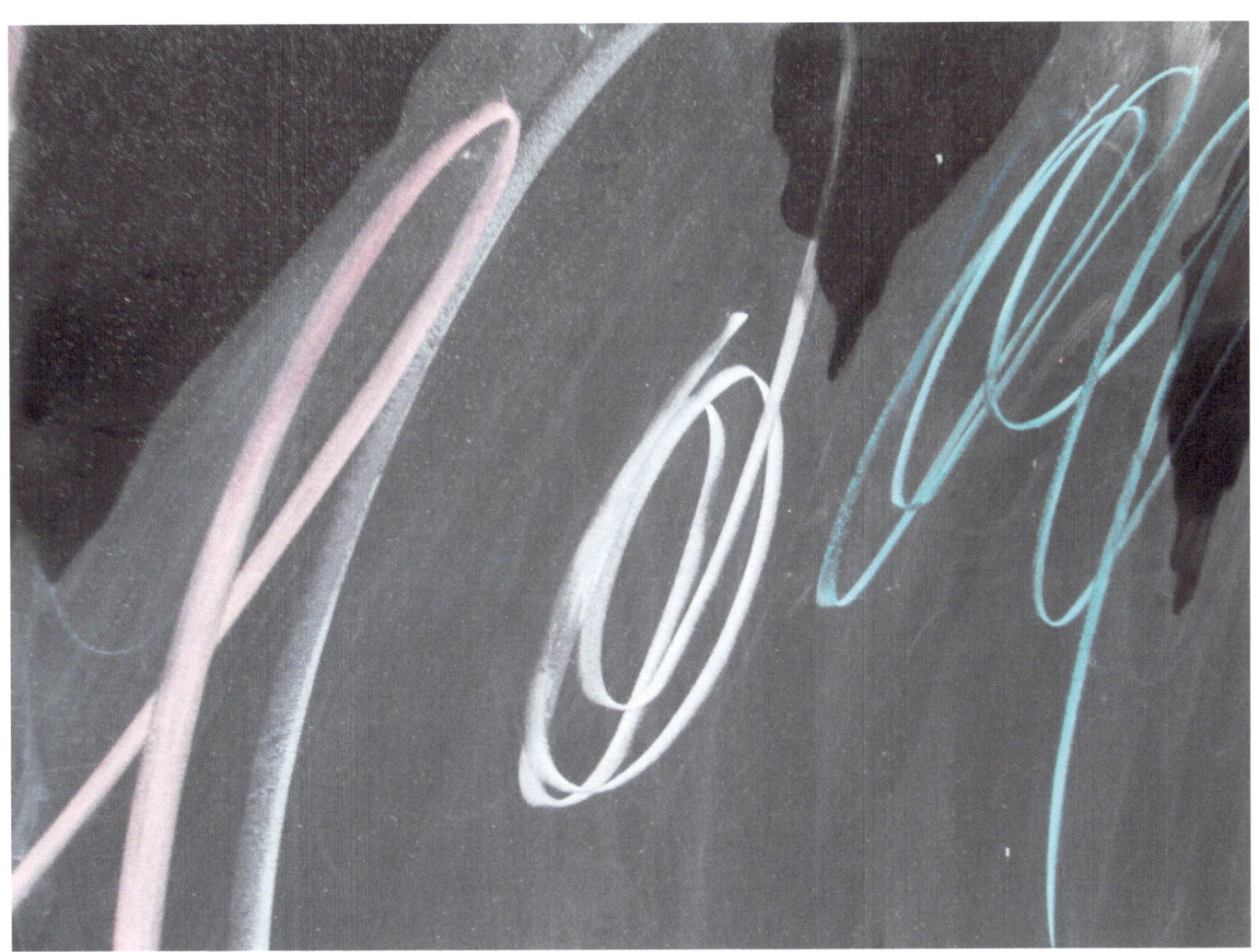

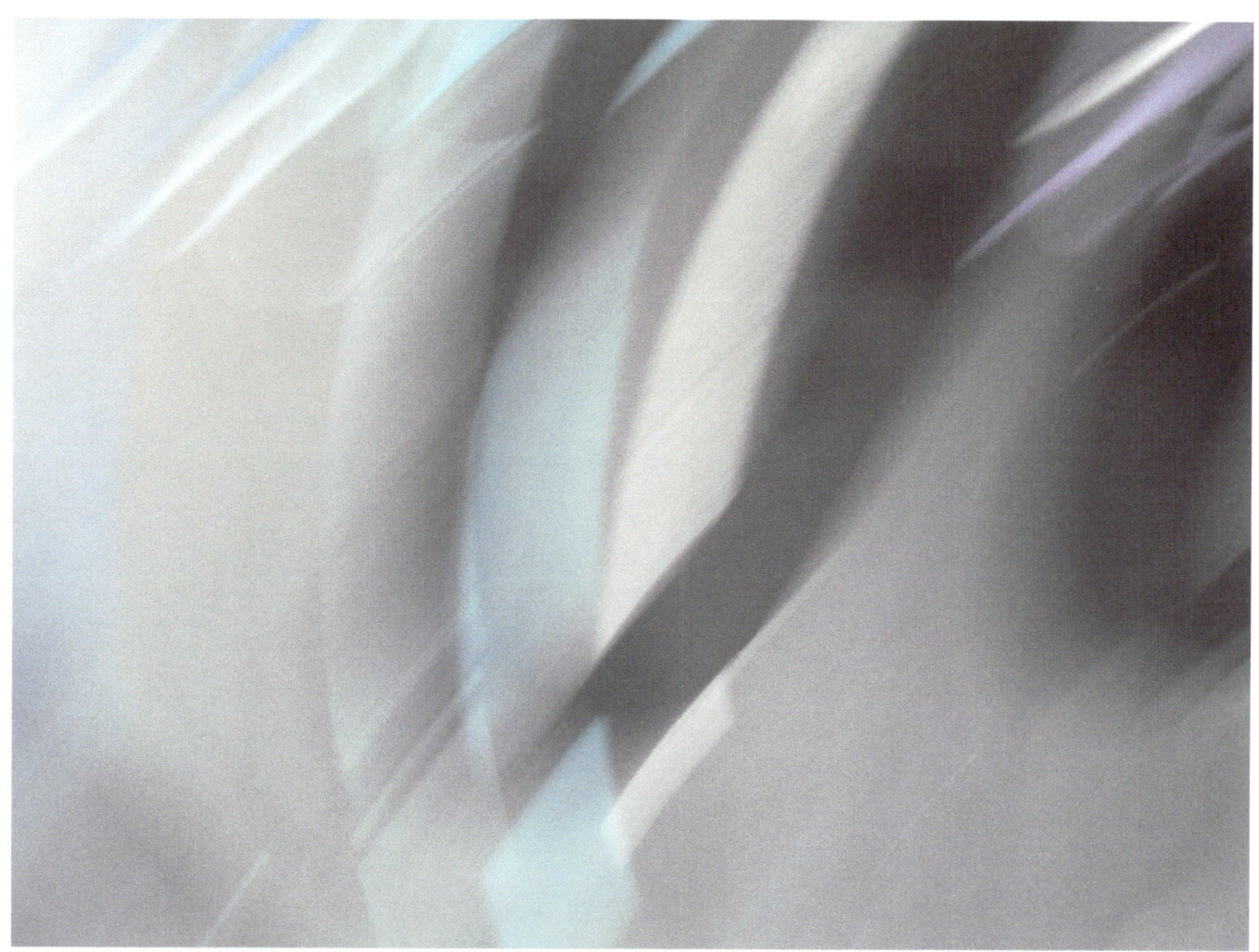

inside my mind
cracking of whips
smoking of a thousand forests
dream mind, dream

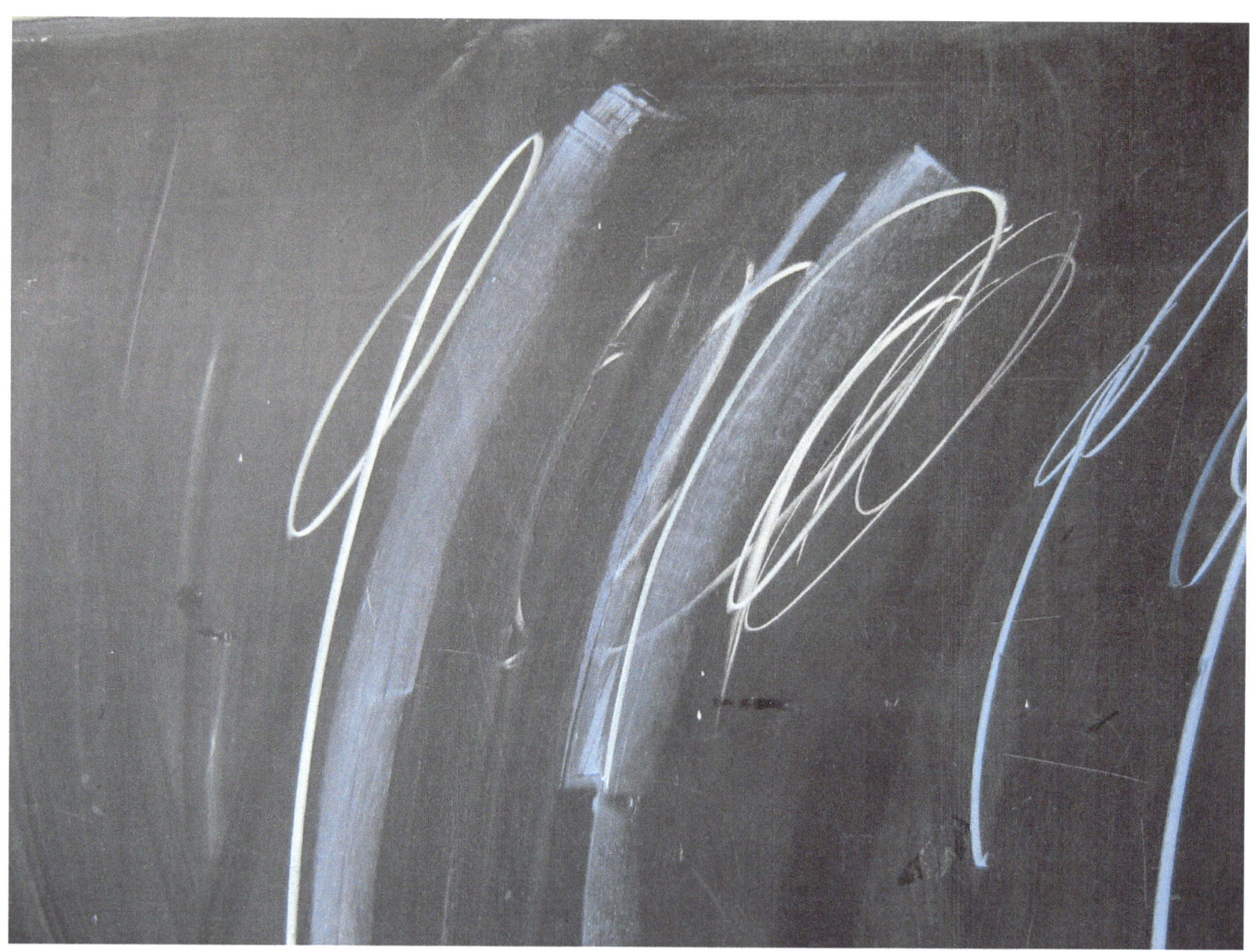

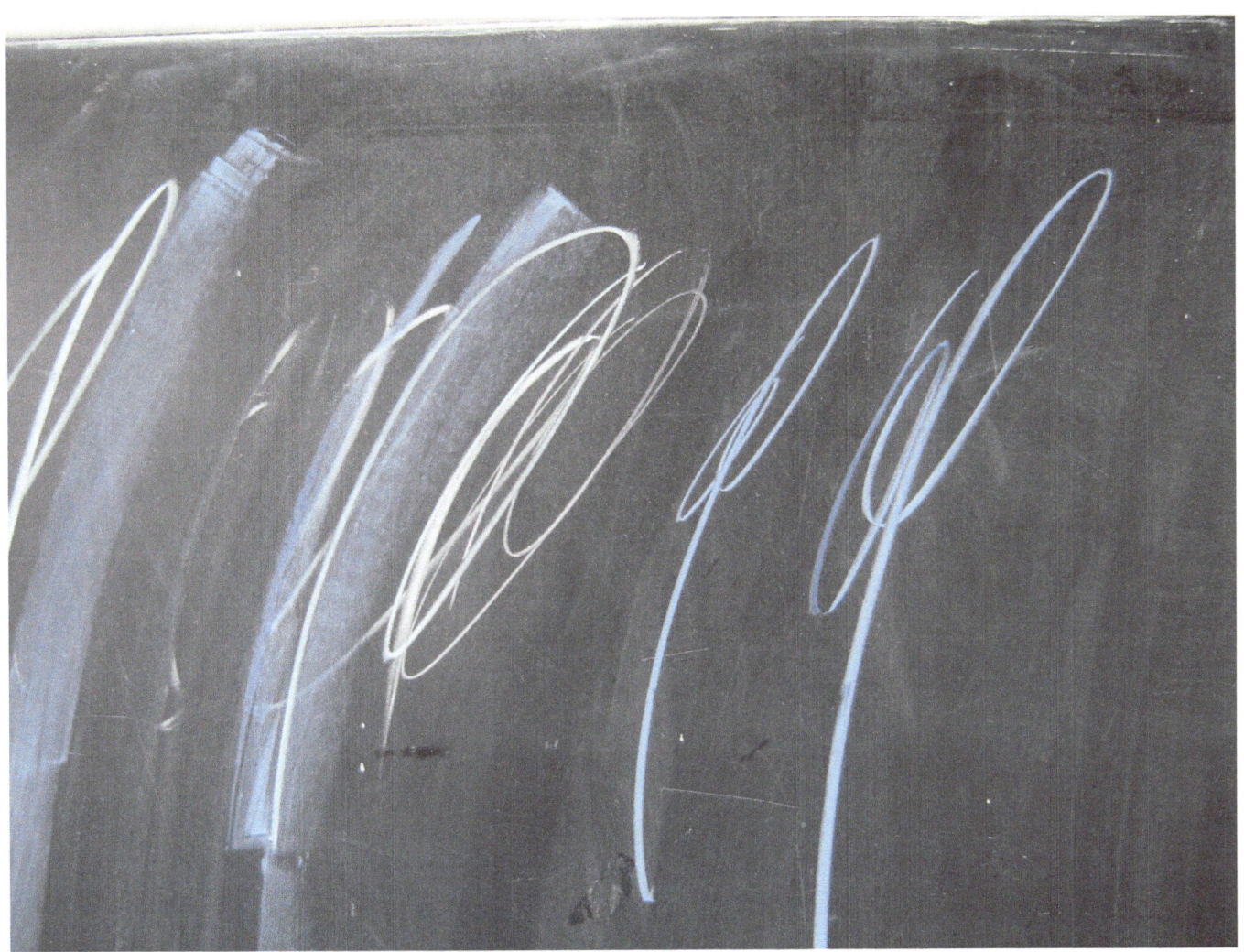

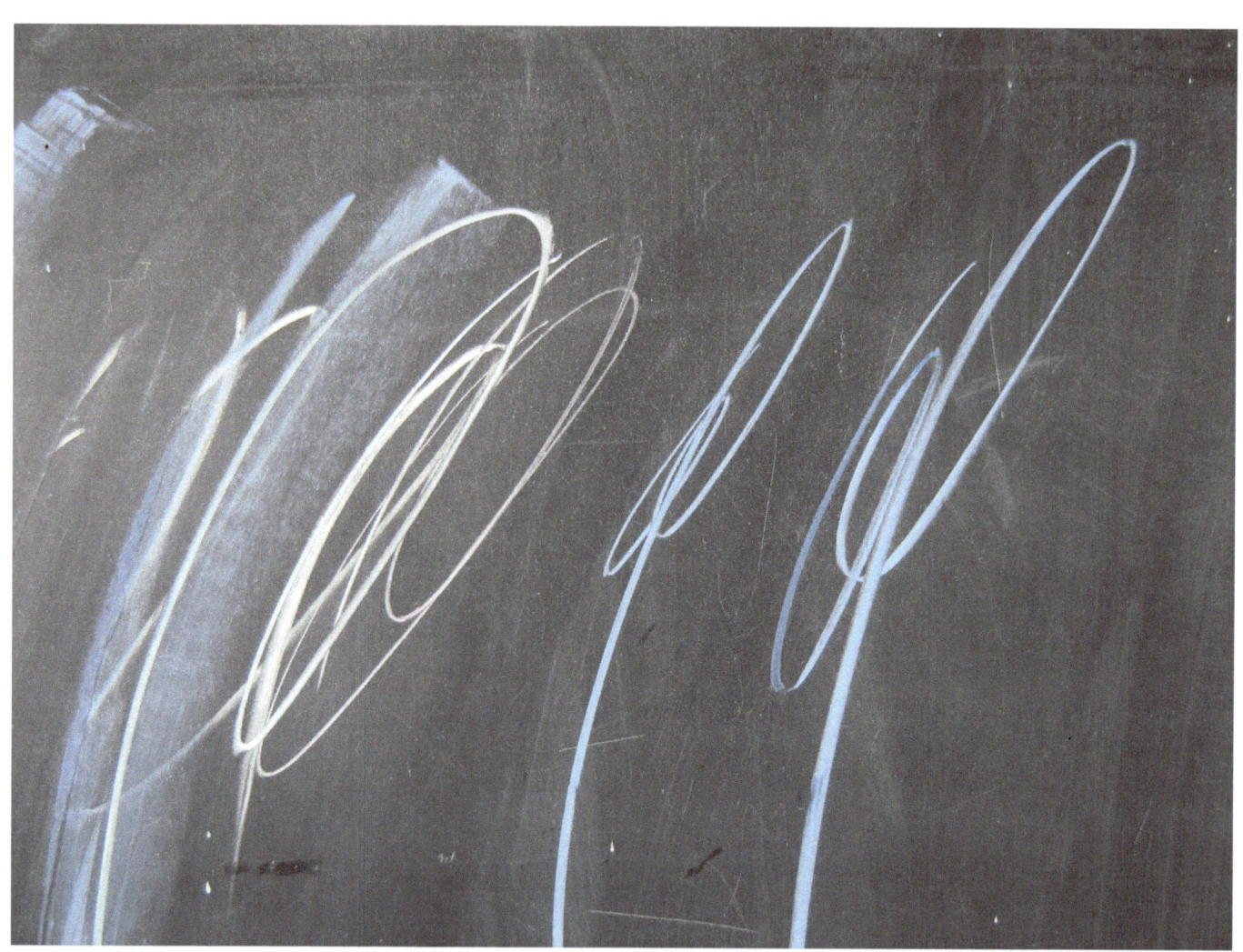

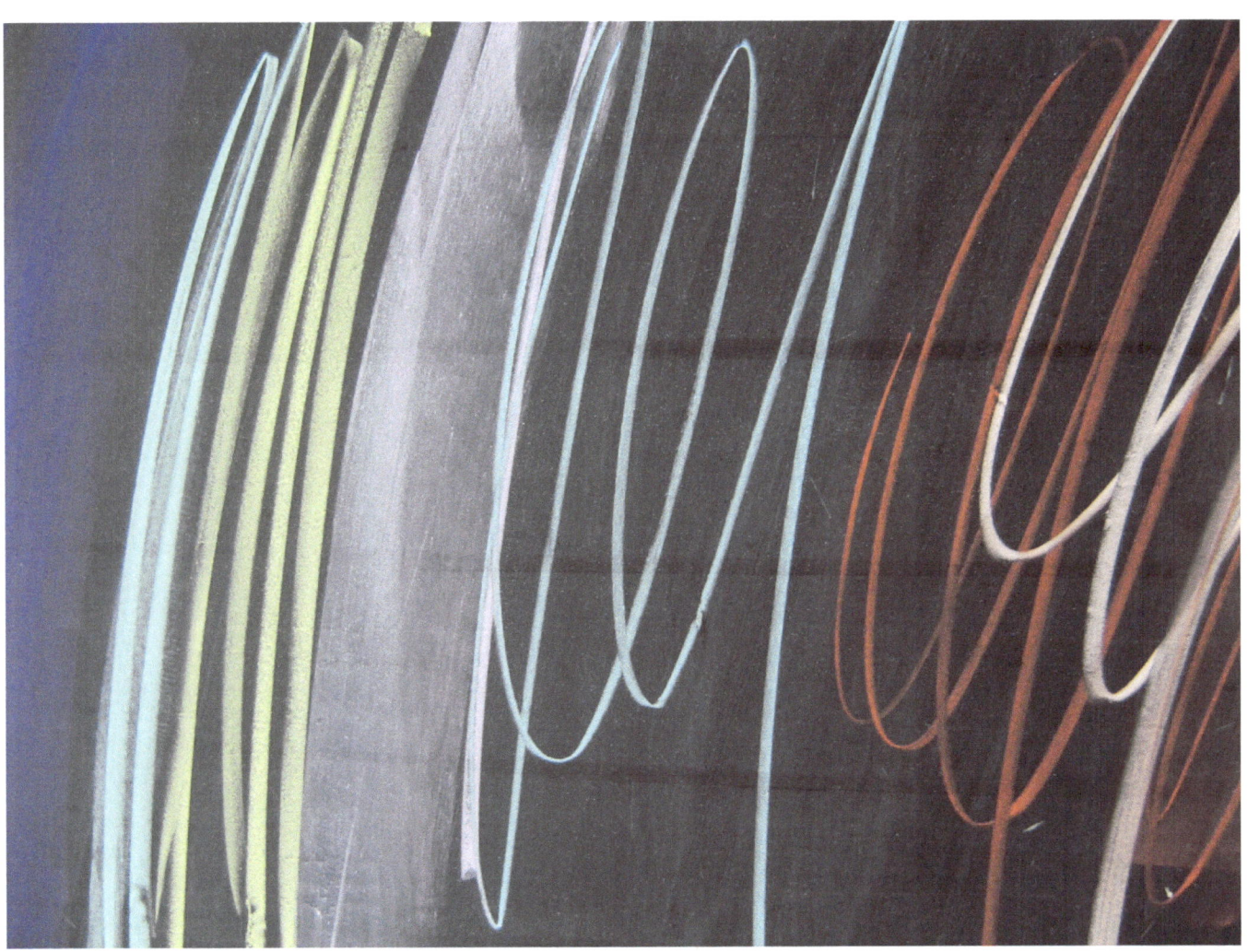

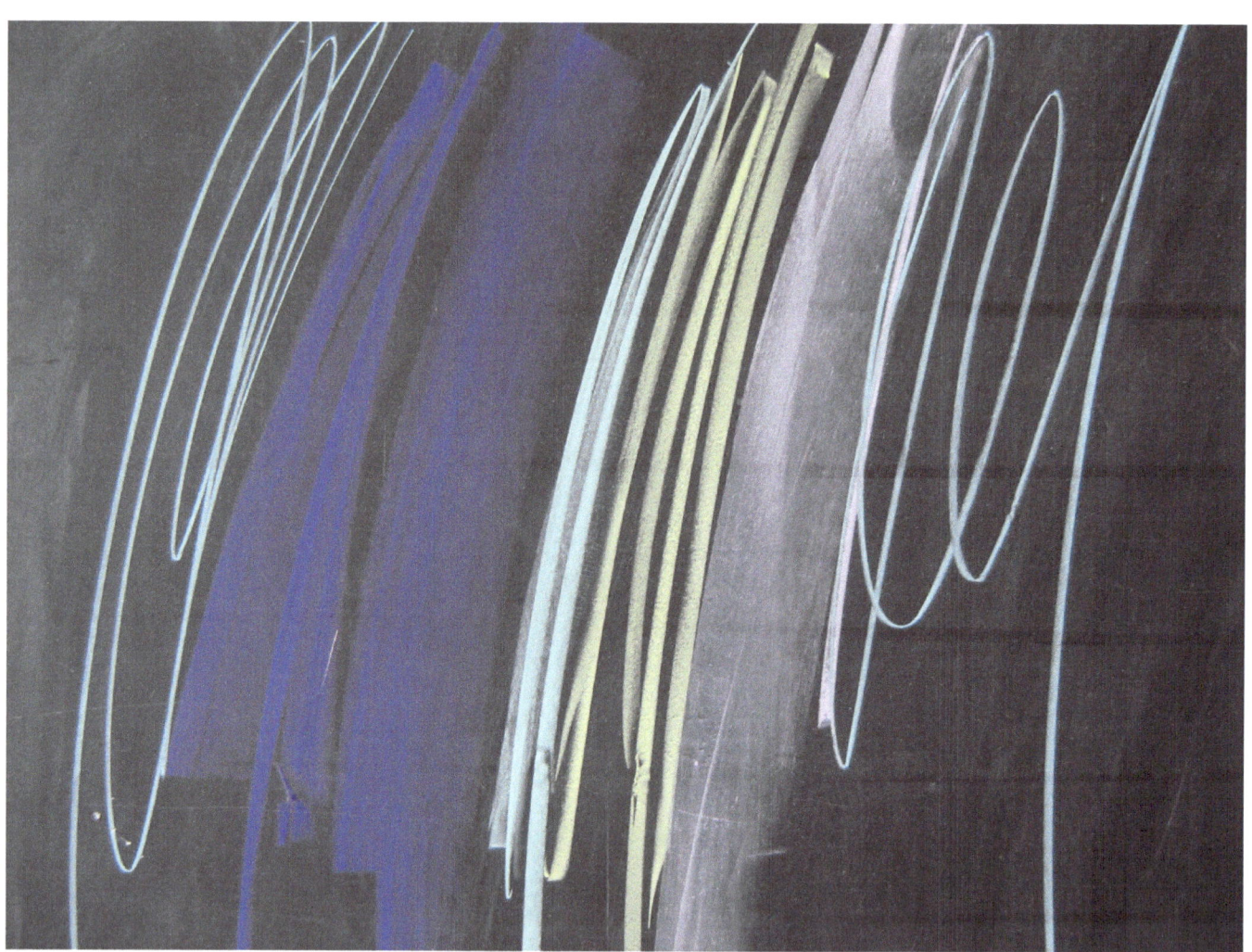

Alaskan freeze
beneath the aurora
quiet Eskimo
summer is forgotten

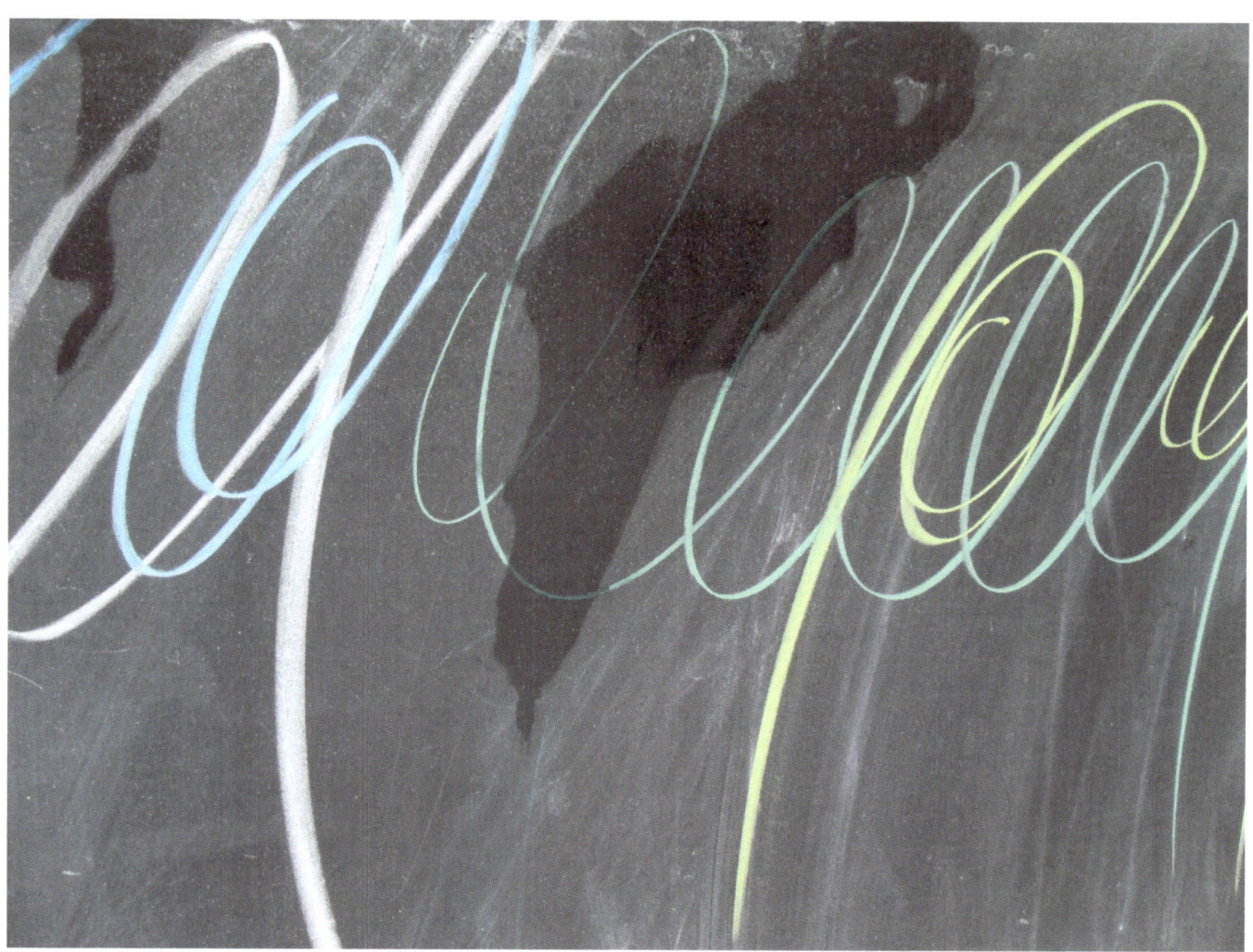

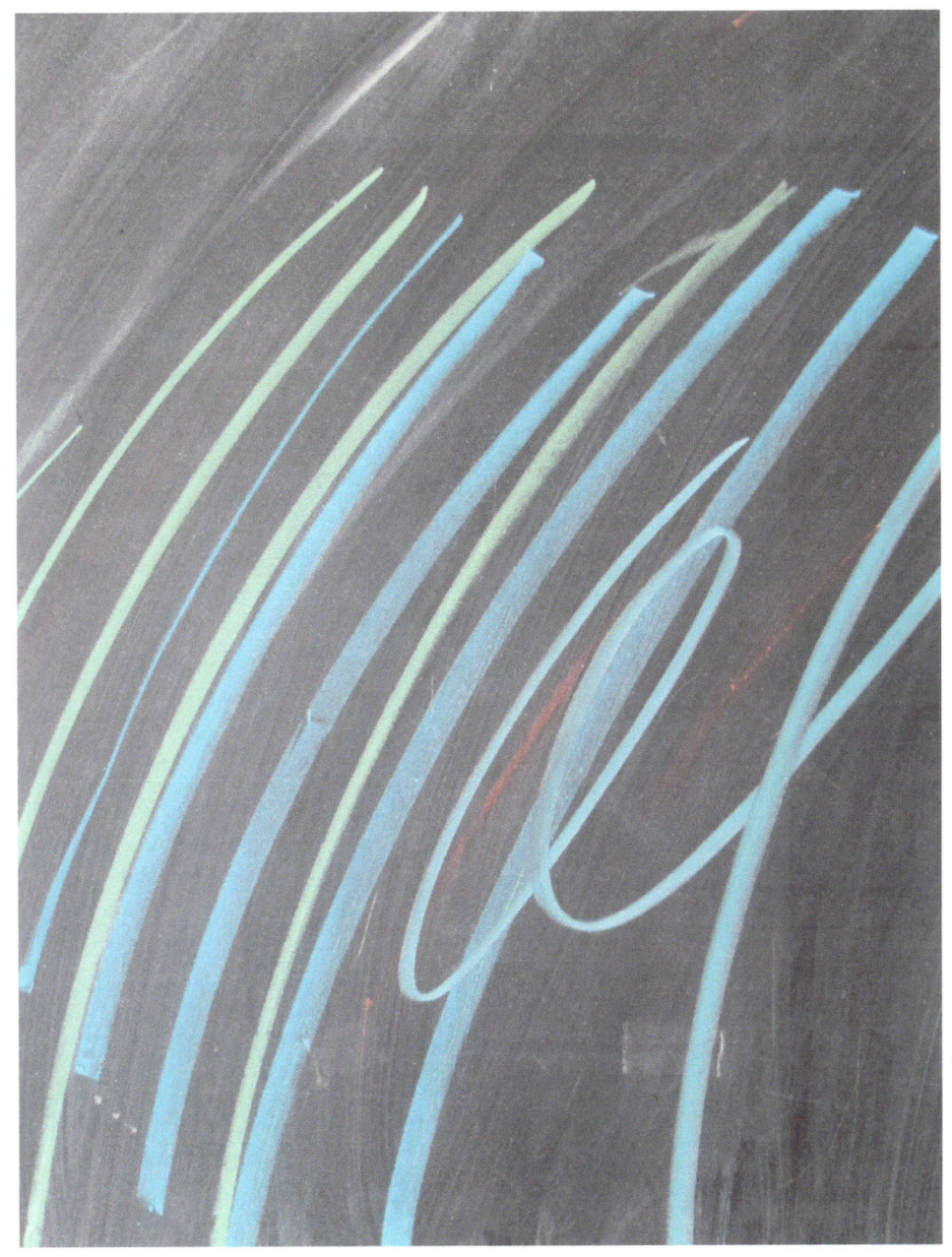

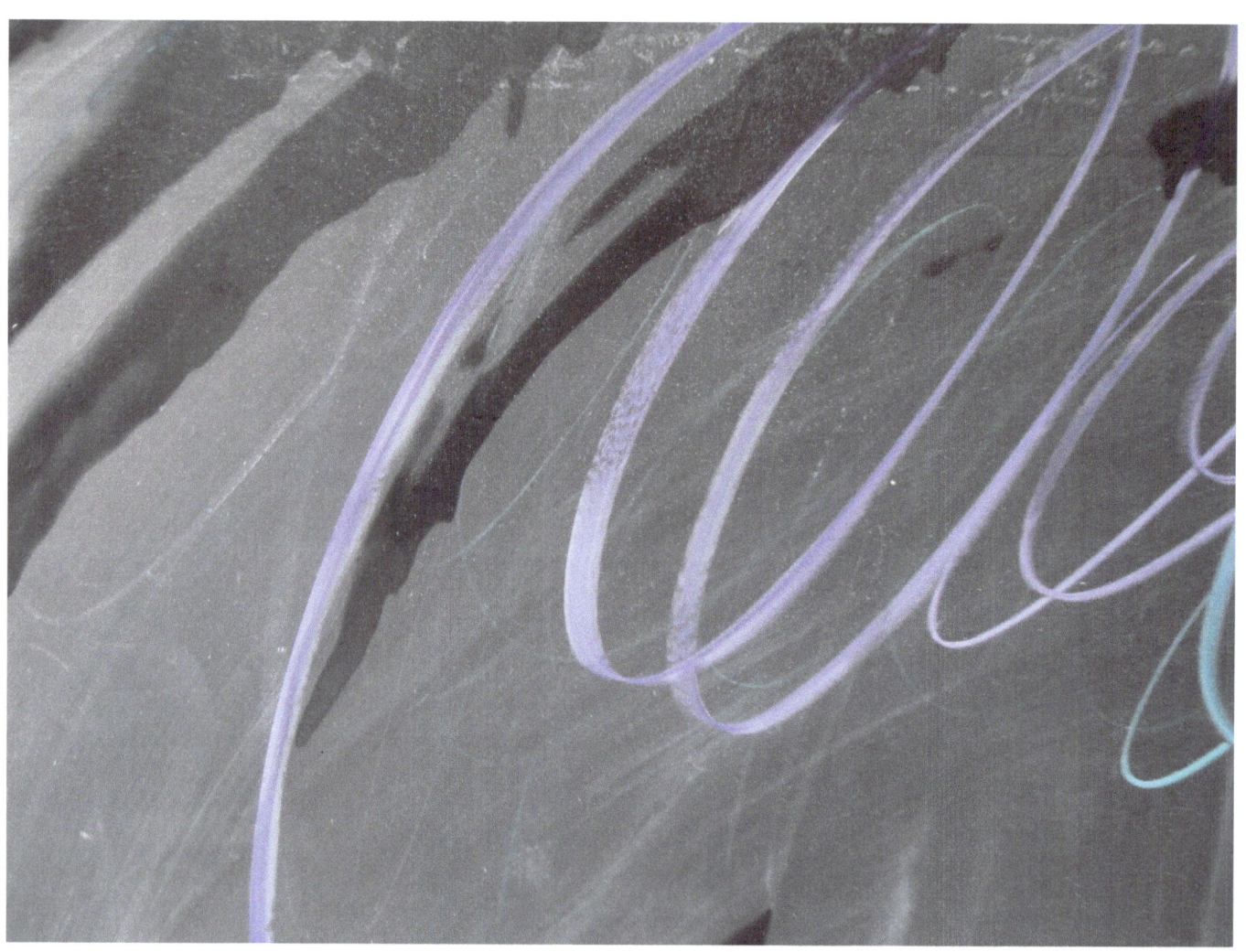

neon lightning
fossilized sand
angel's anger
becomes glass

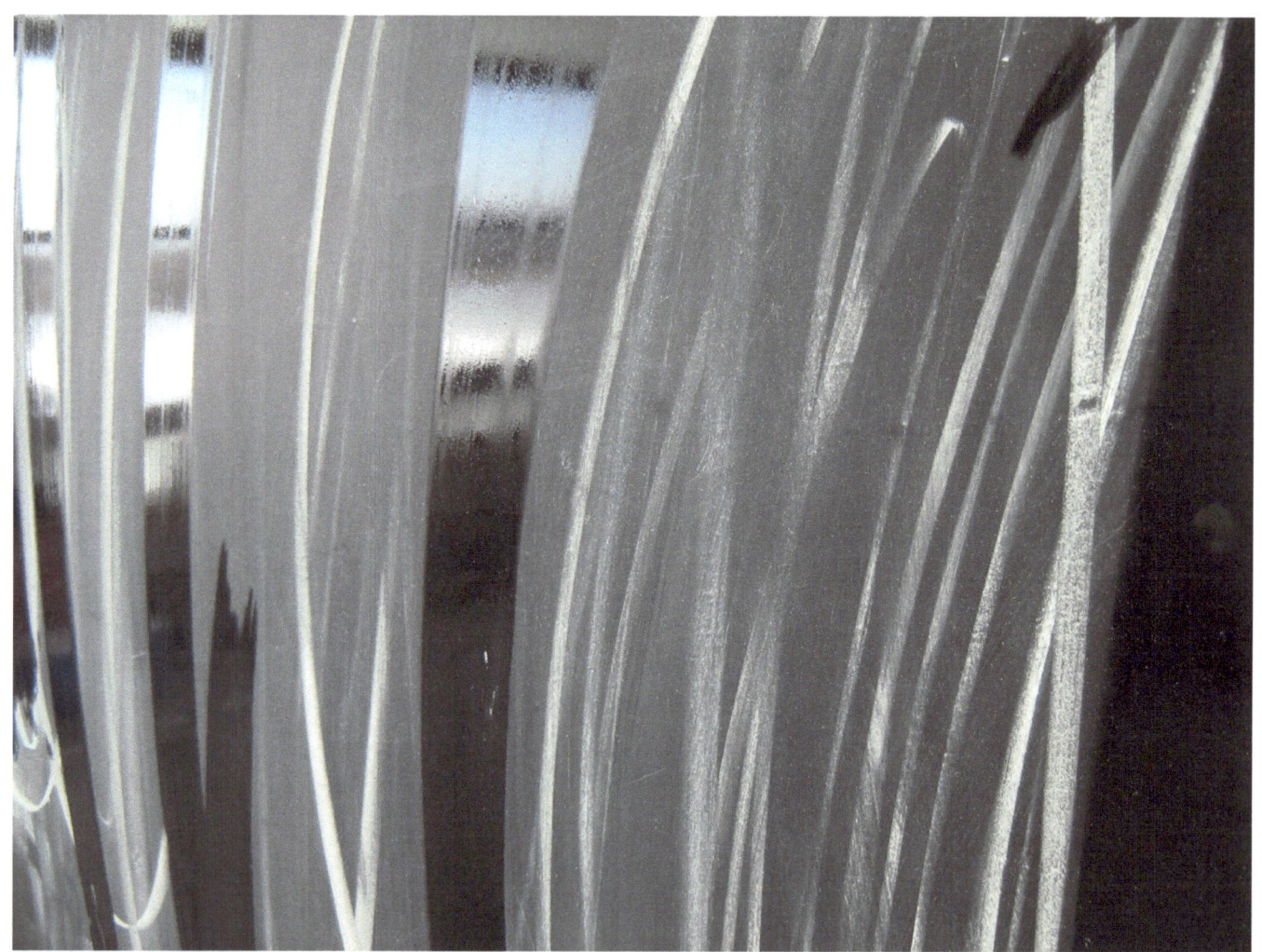

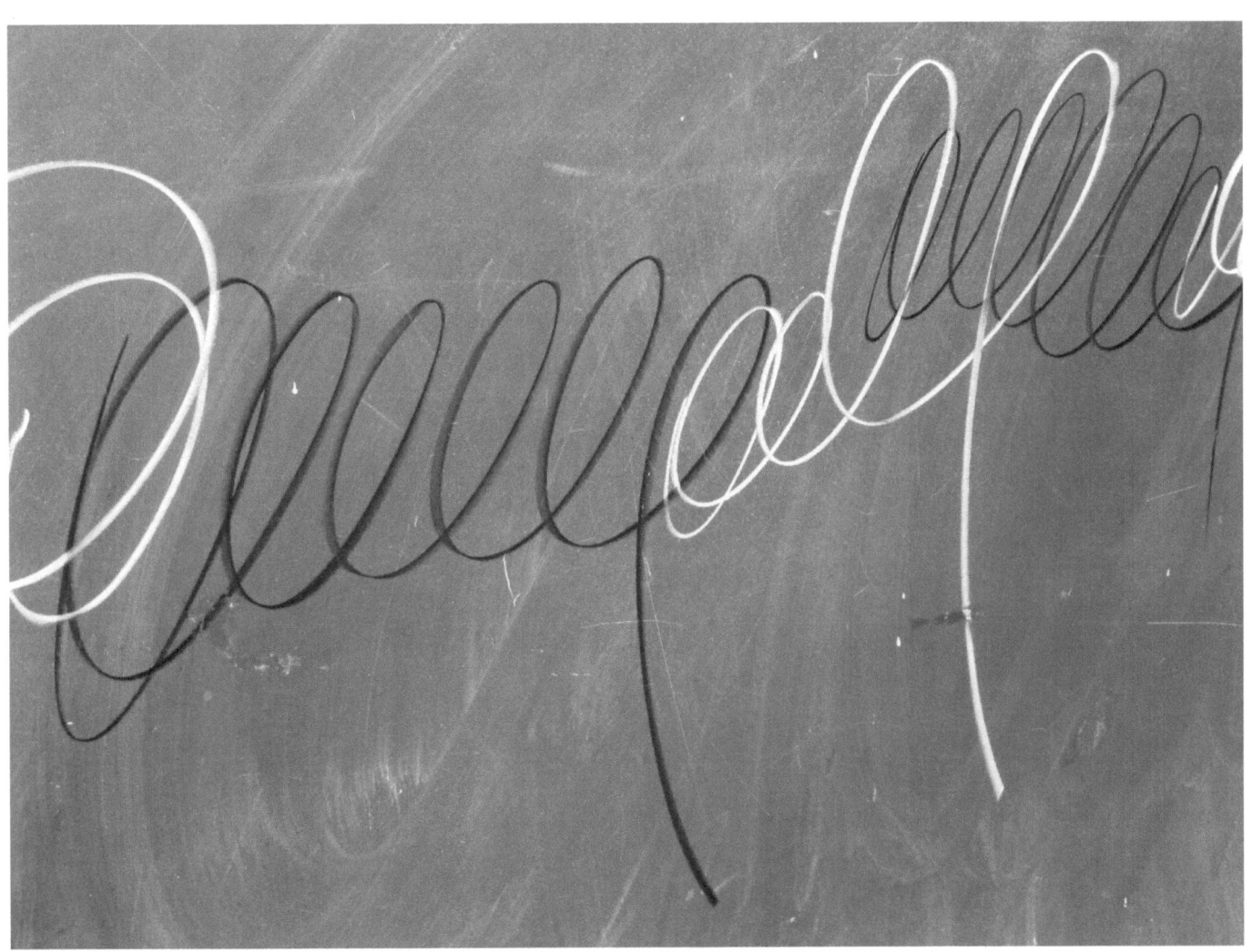

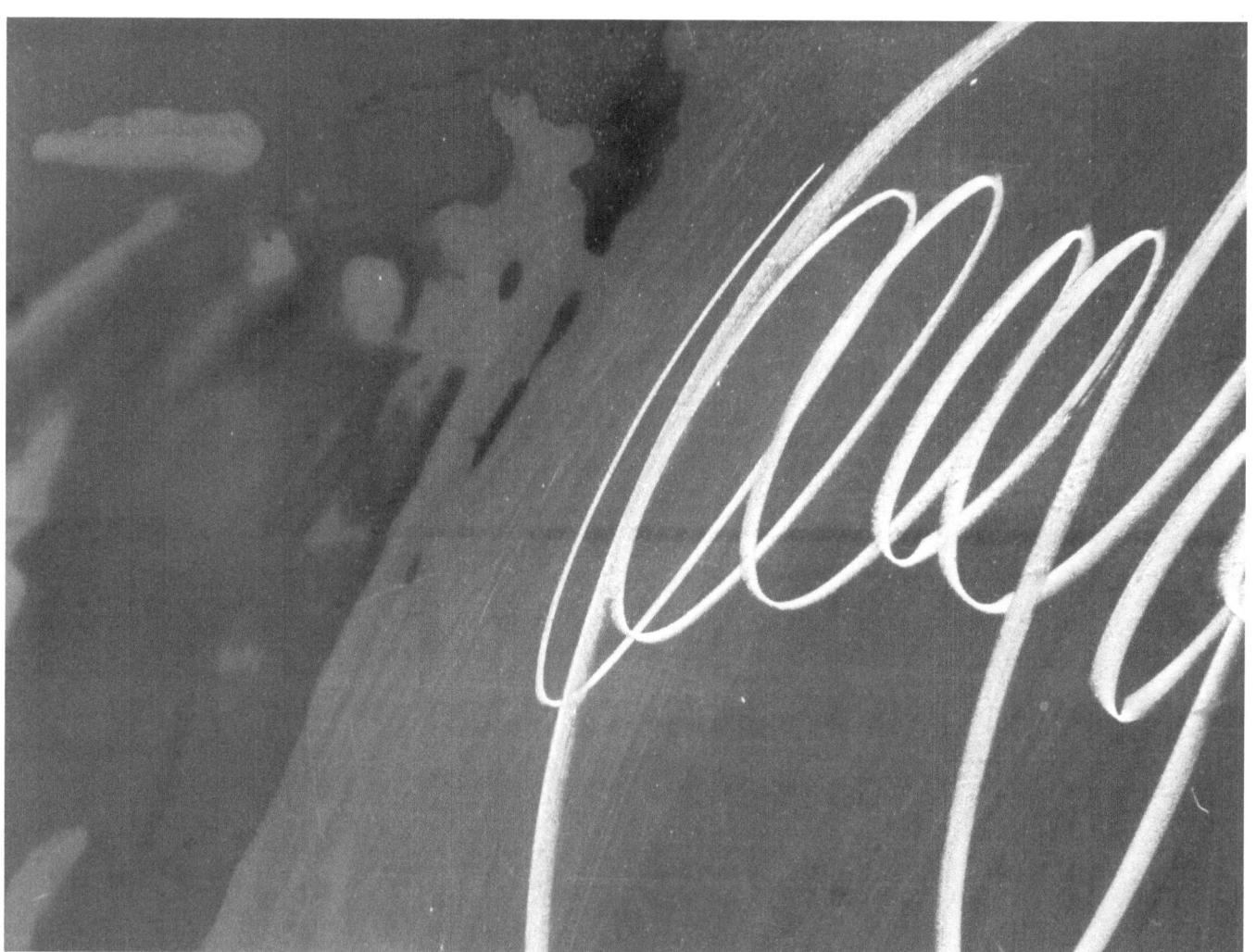

melancholic saint
a black phantom
candlelight spurs his hope

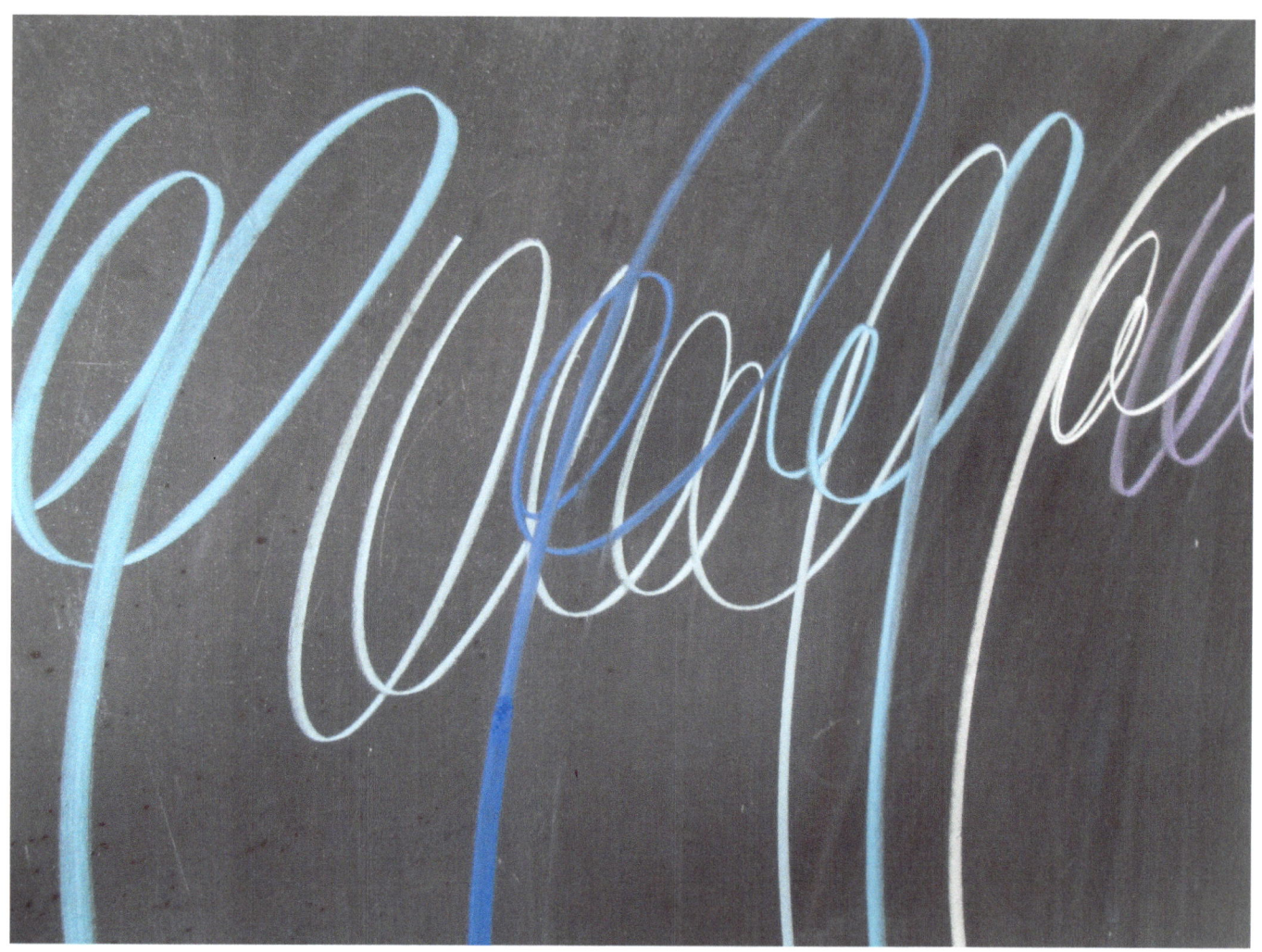

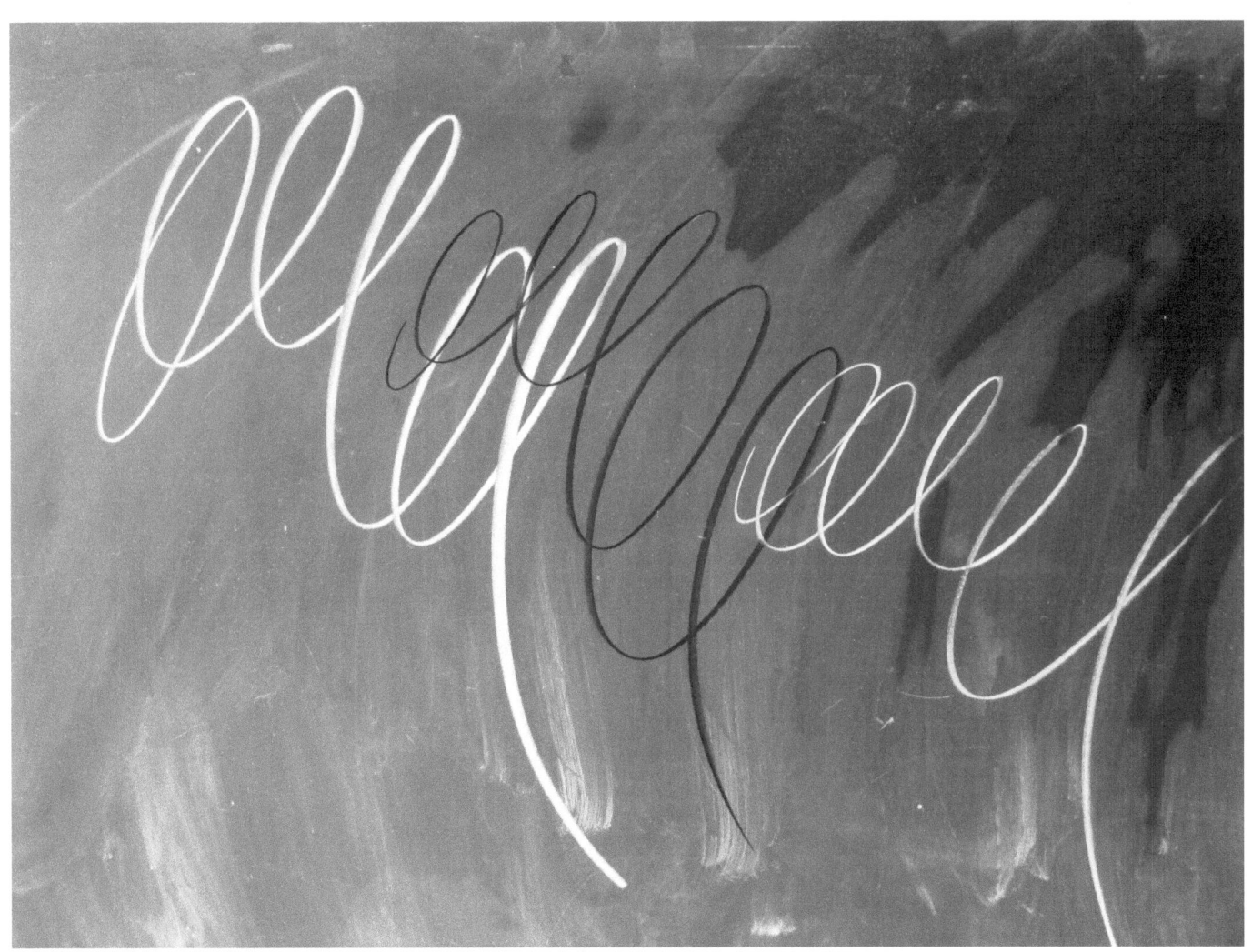

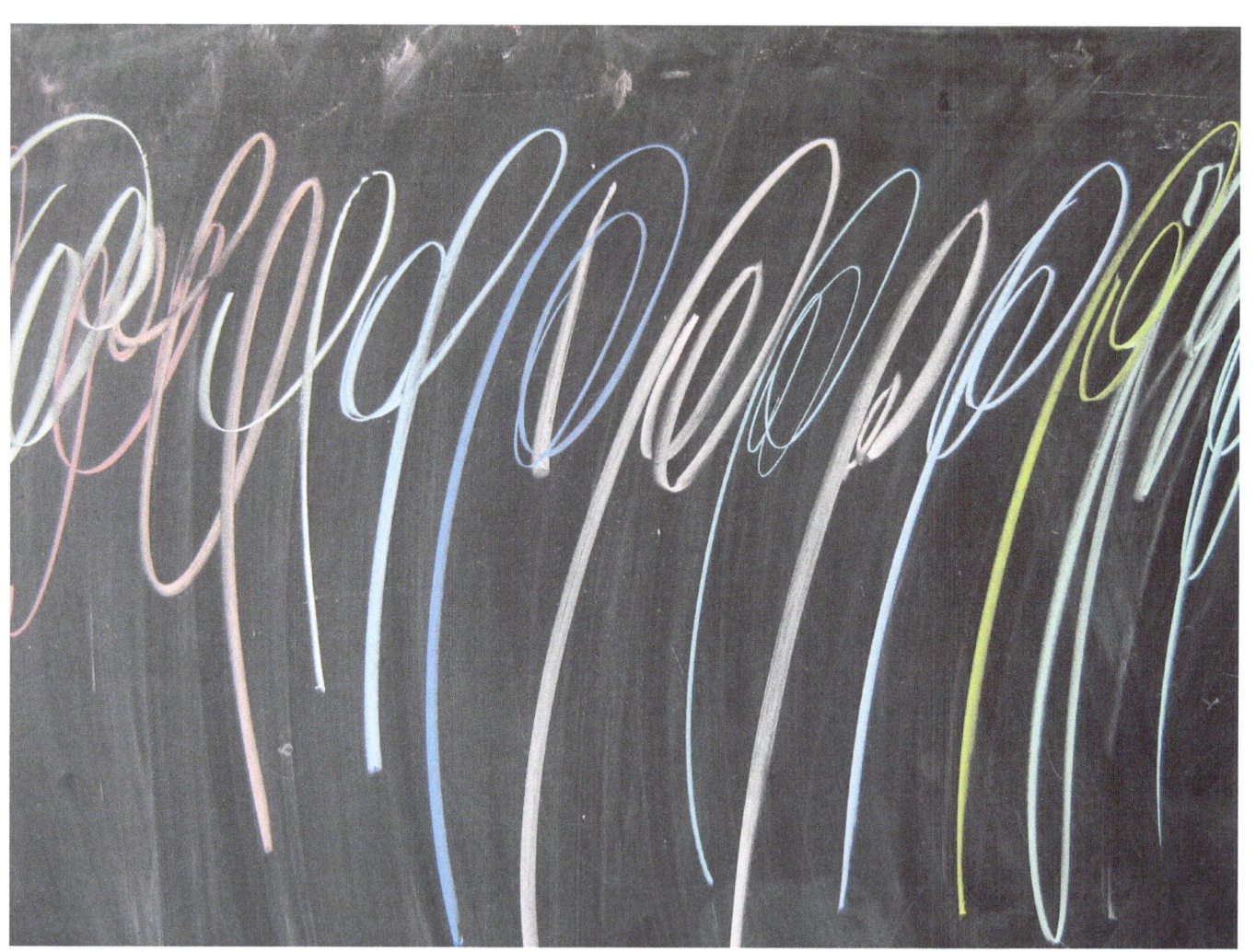

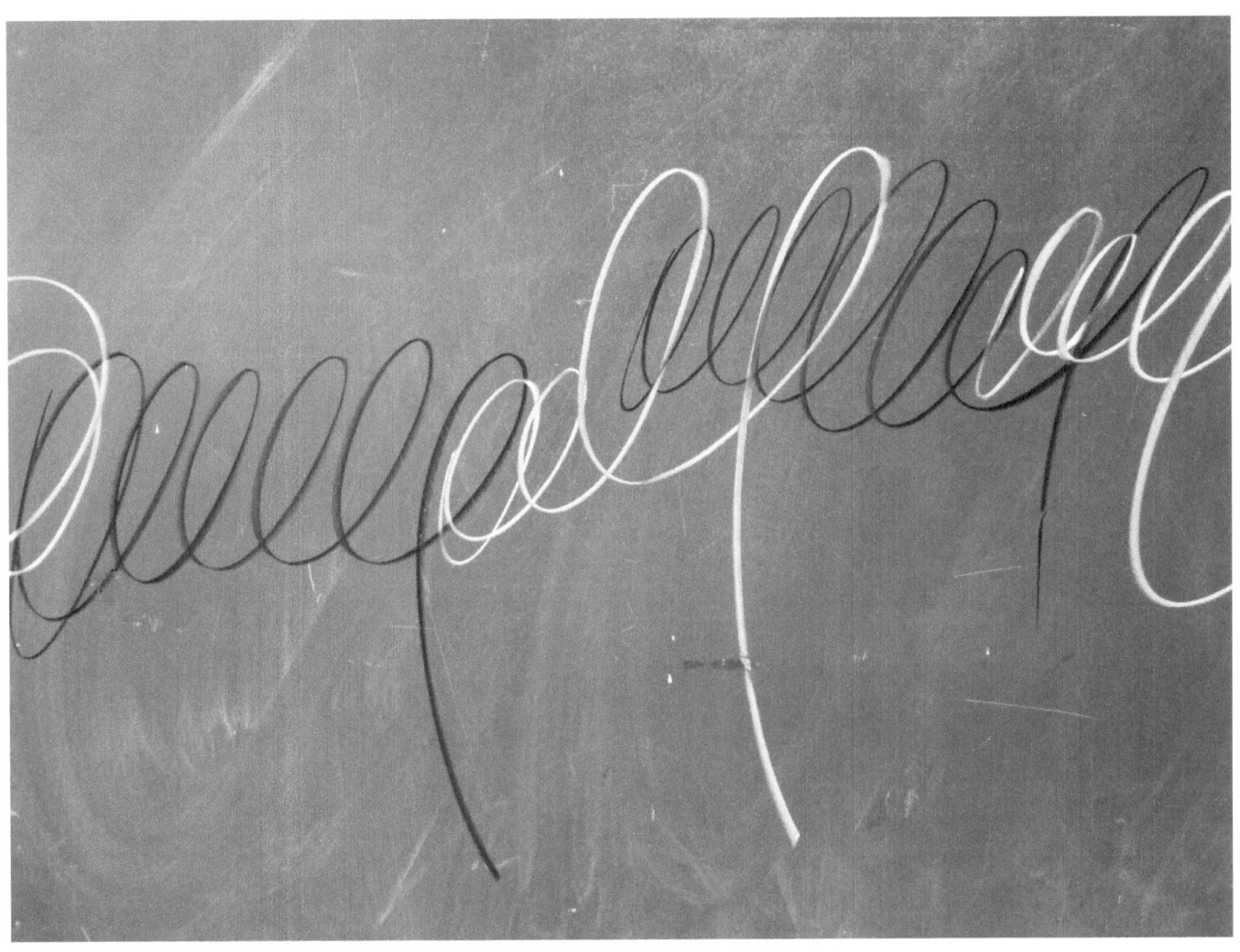

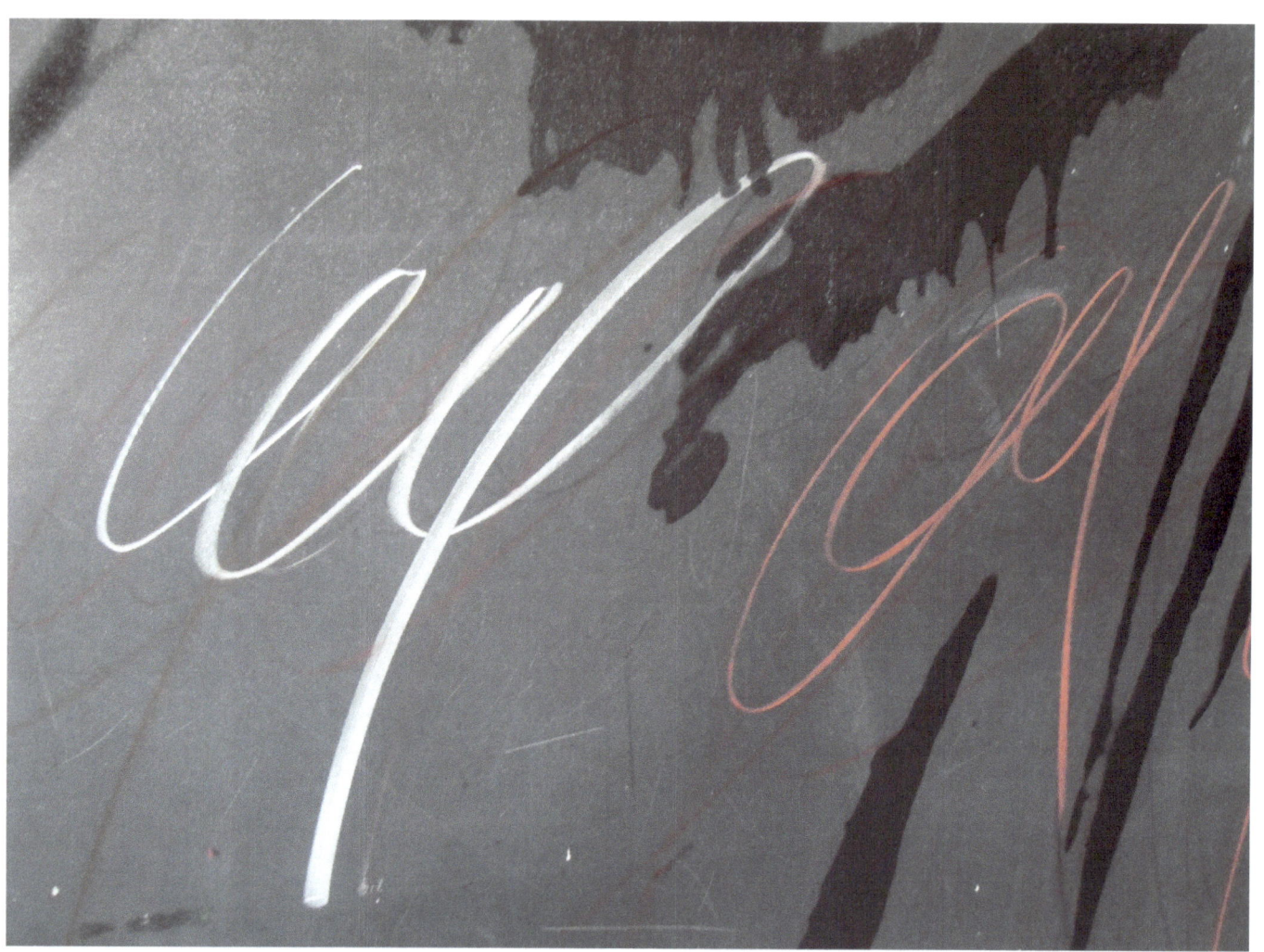

tempestuous love
absolute anguish
you are with me

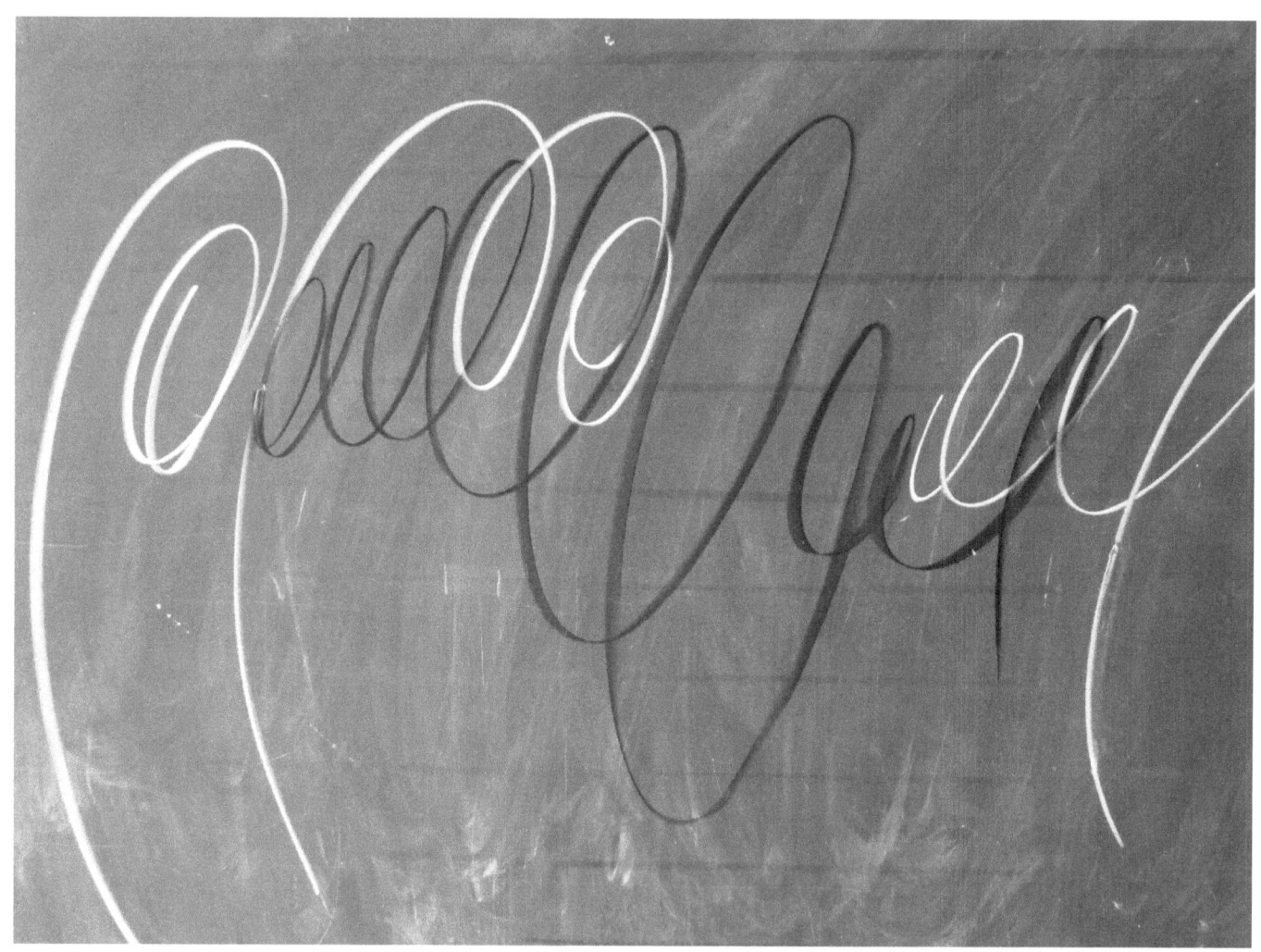

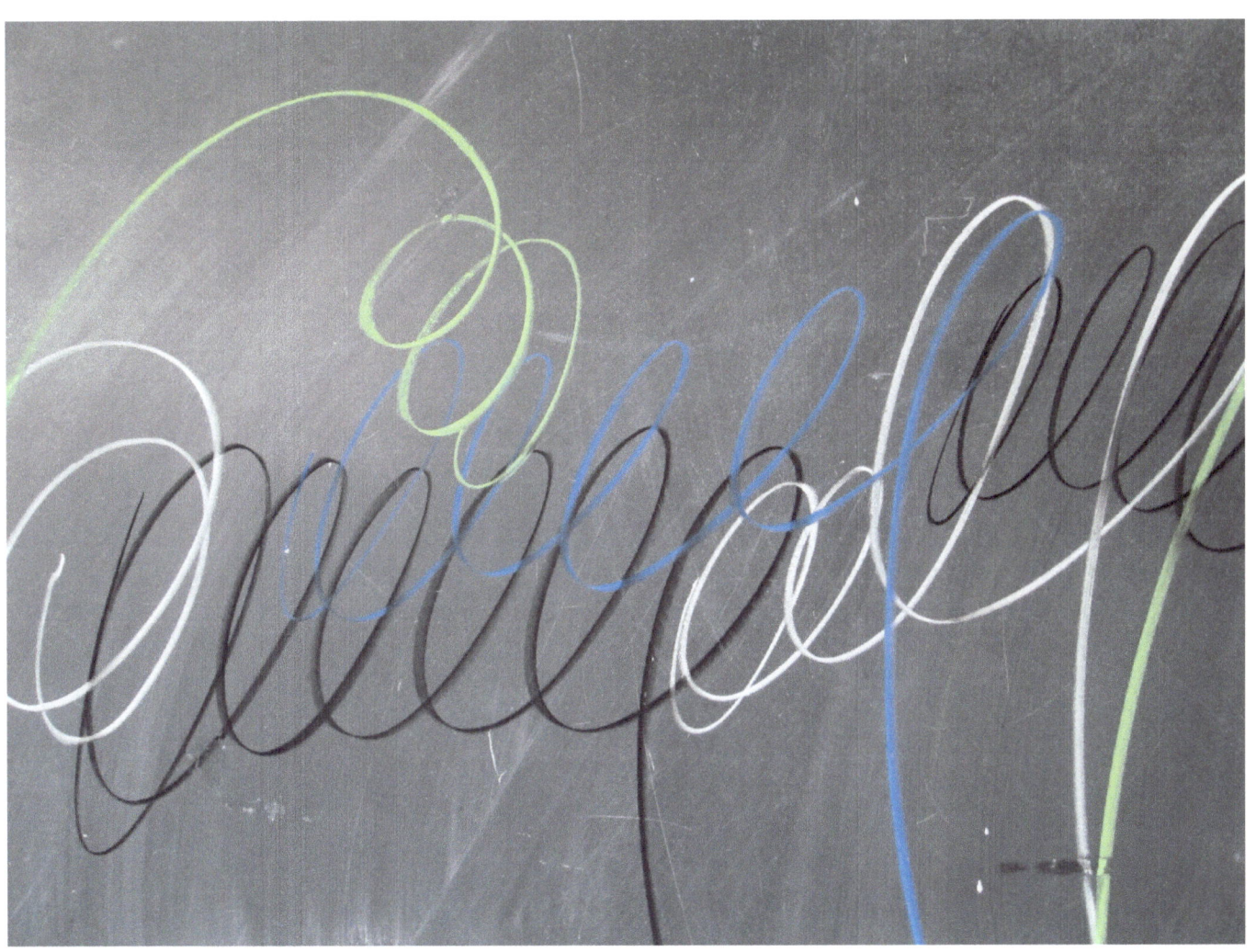

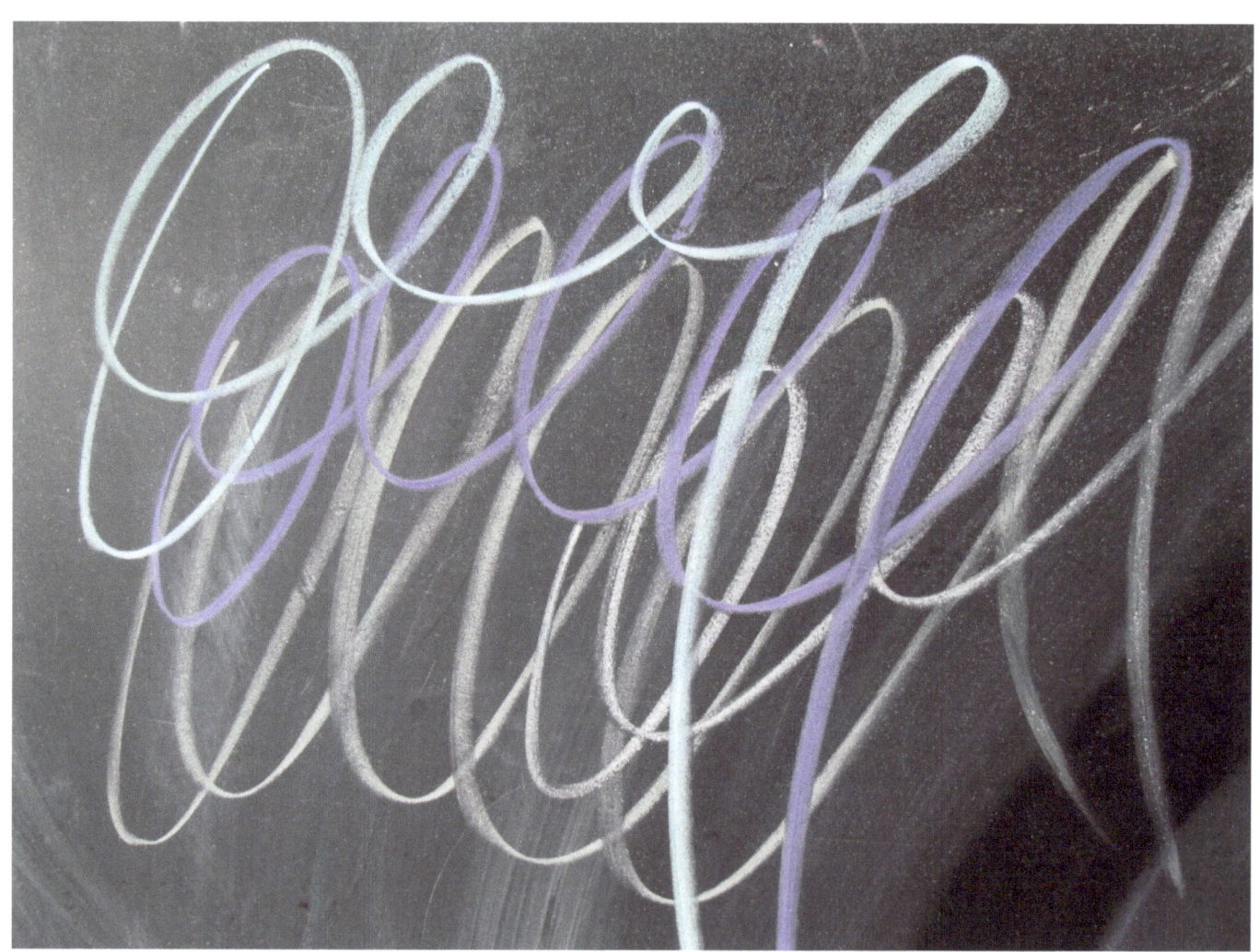

eight eyed spider weaving tapestries
all seeing Panoptes awake for eternity
archangel Azrael messenger of souls
nature becomes myth becomes religion becomes void

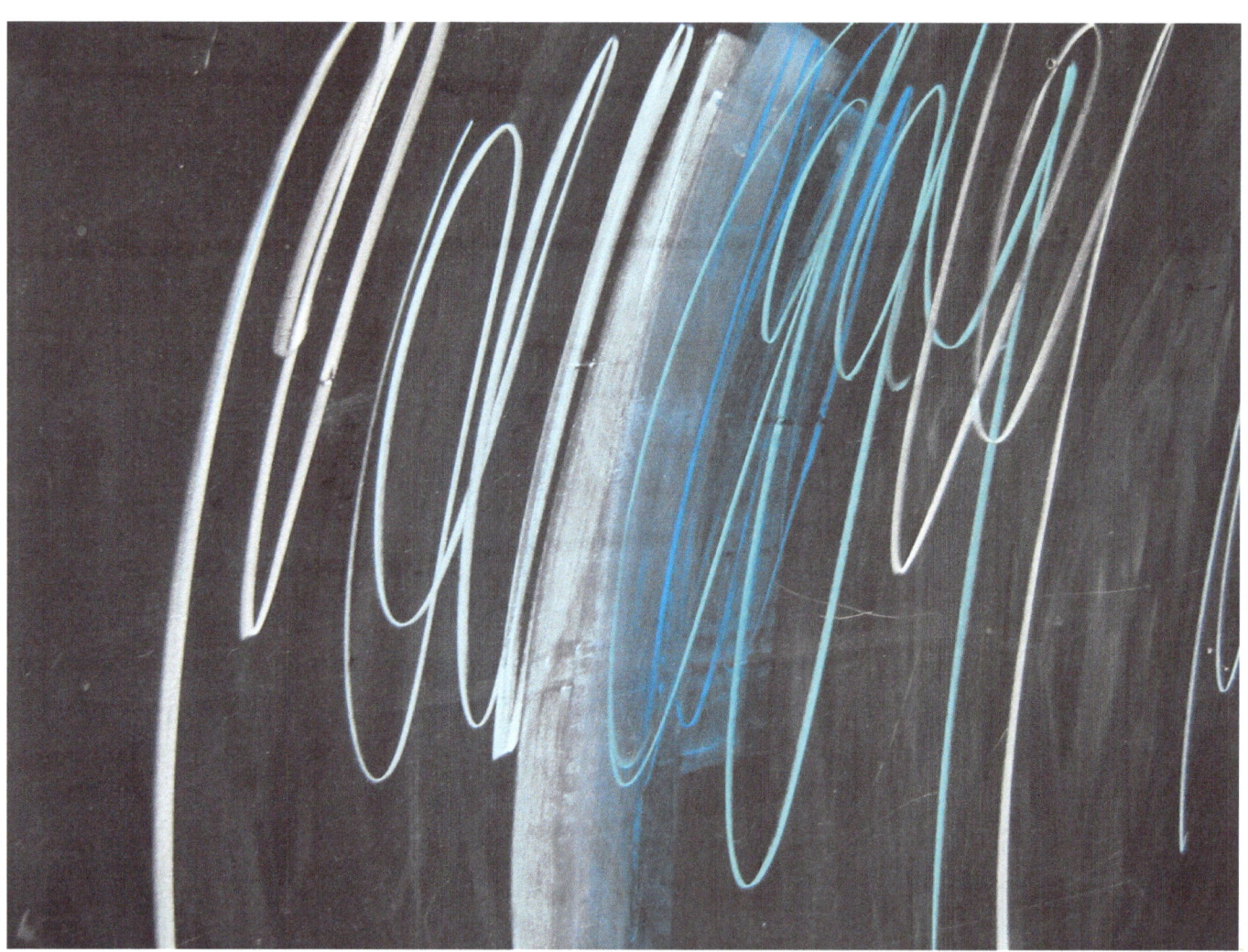

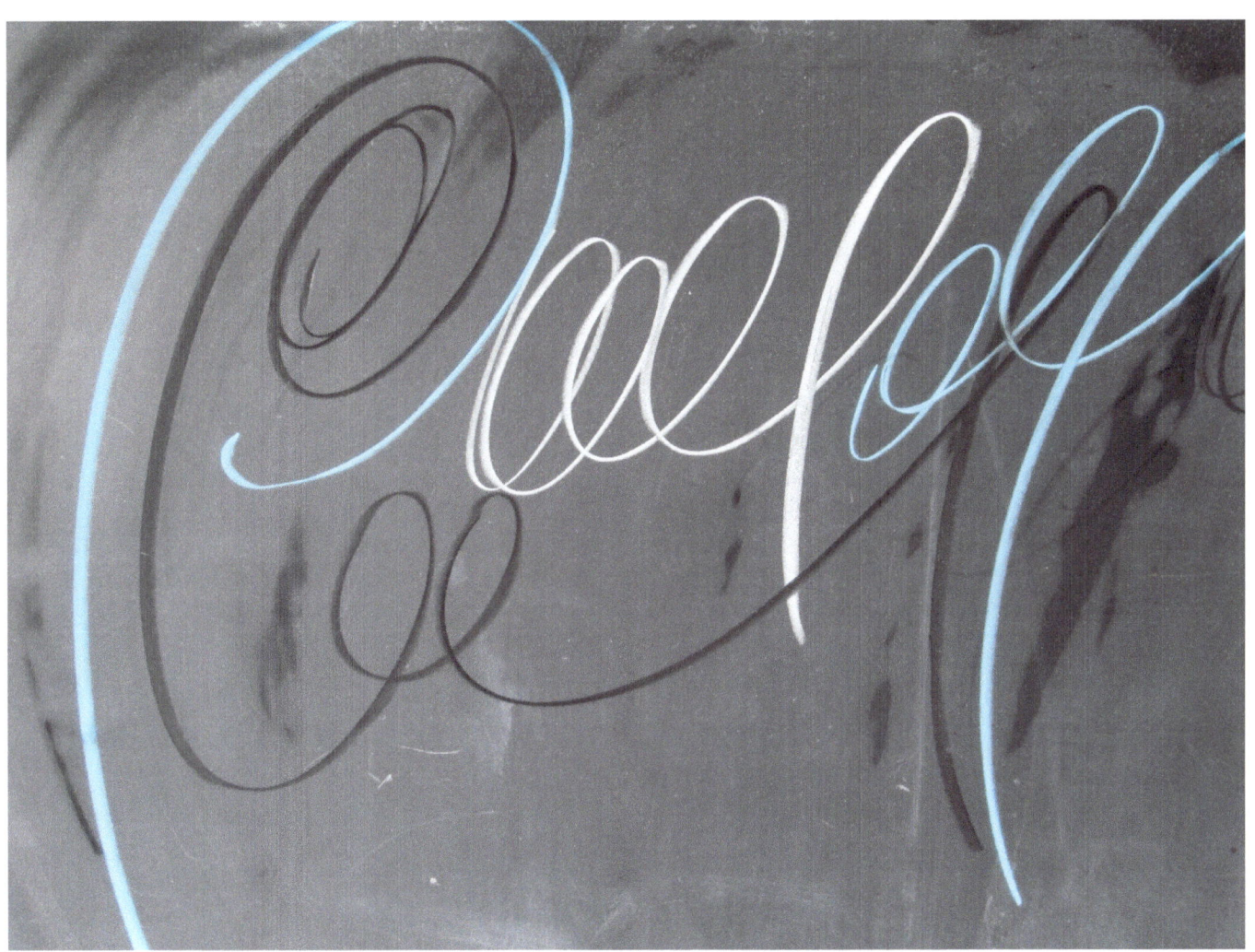

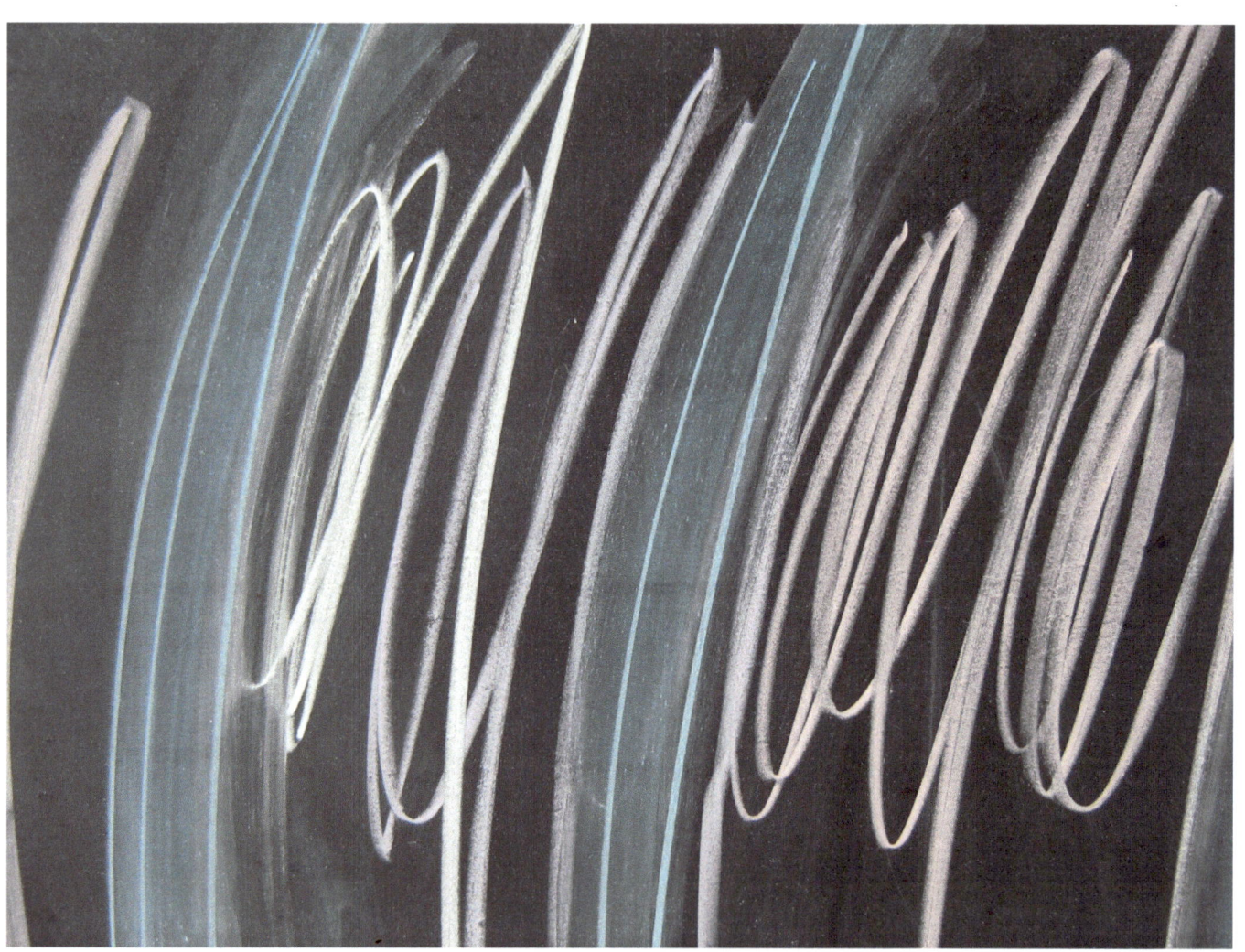

out at sea
the waves crumble
my skin trembles
there is no place calmer
yet,
I ask for nature's mercy

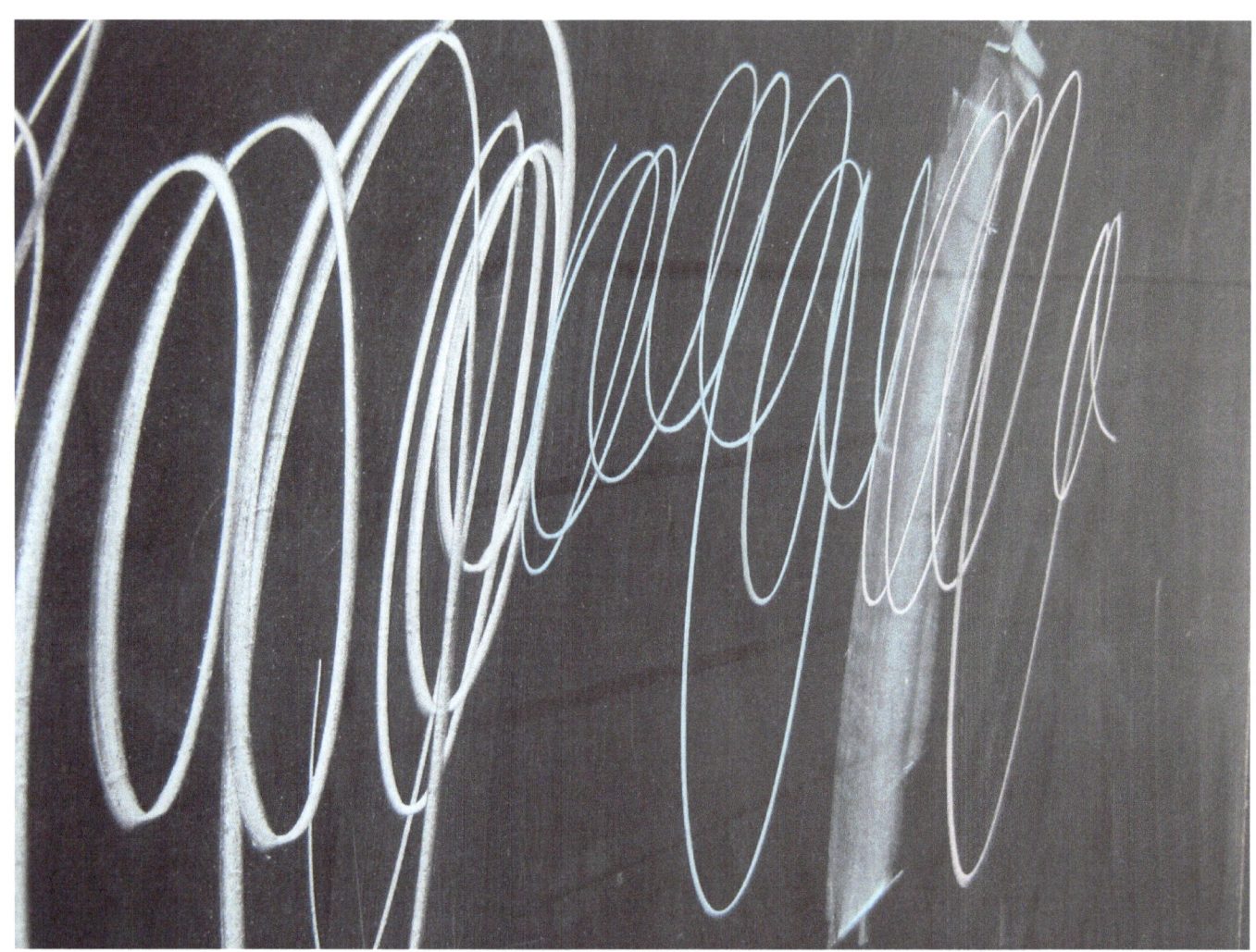

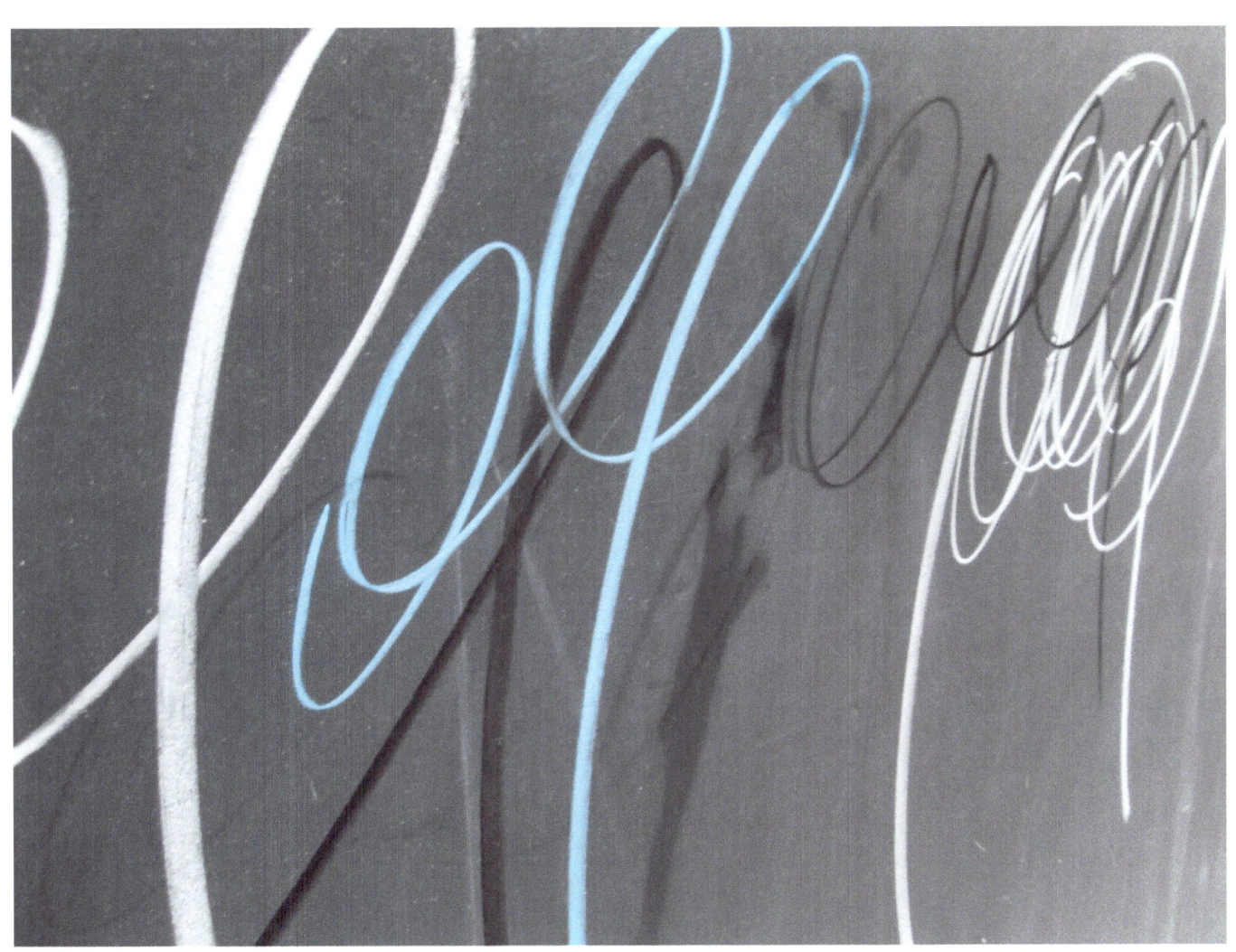

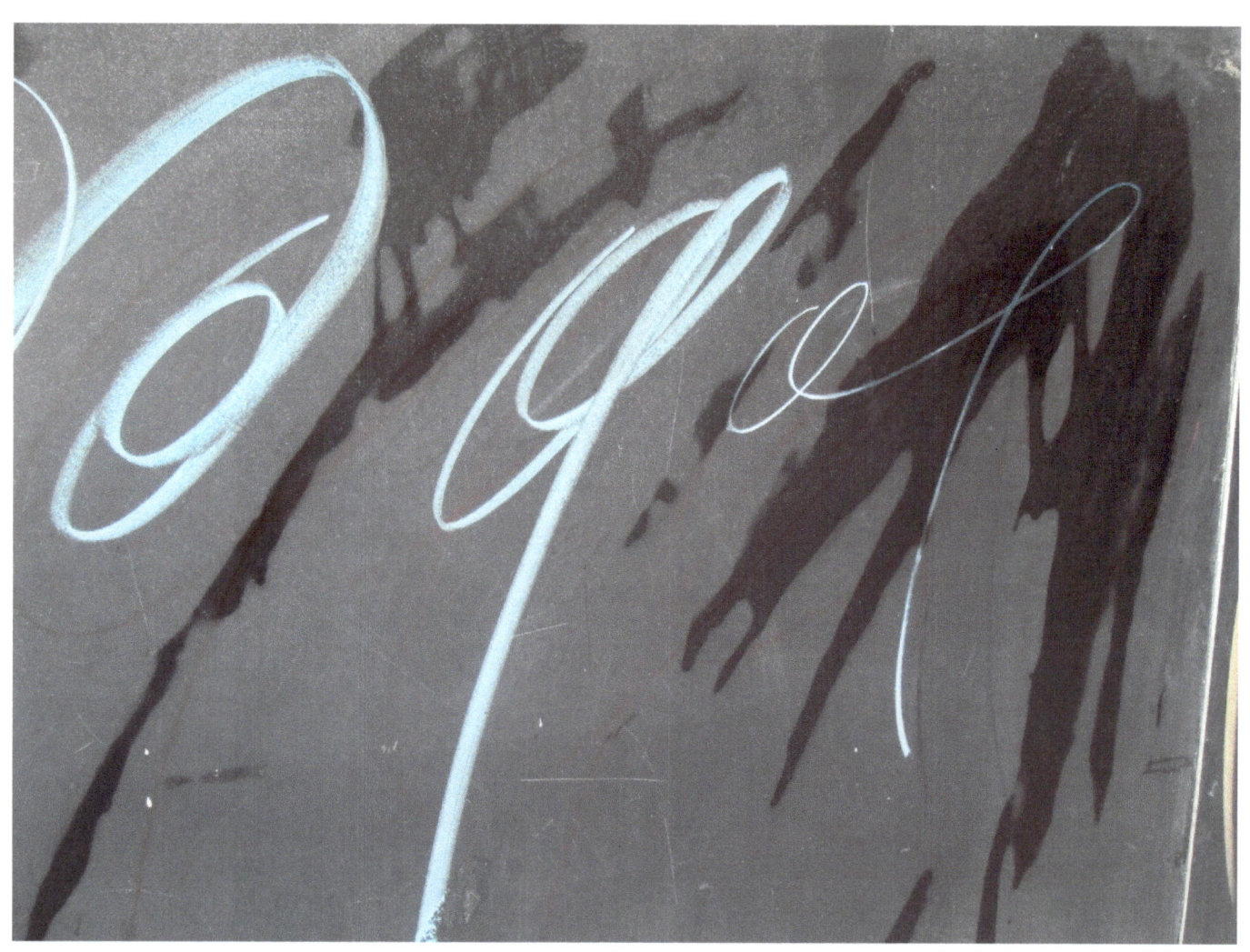

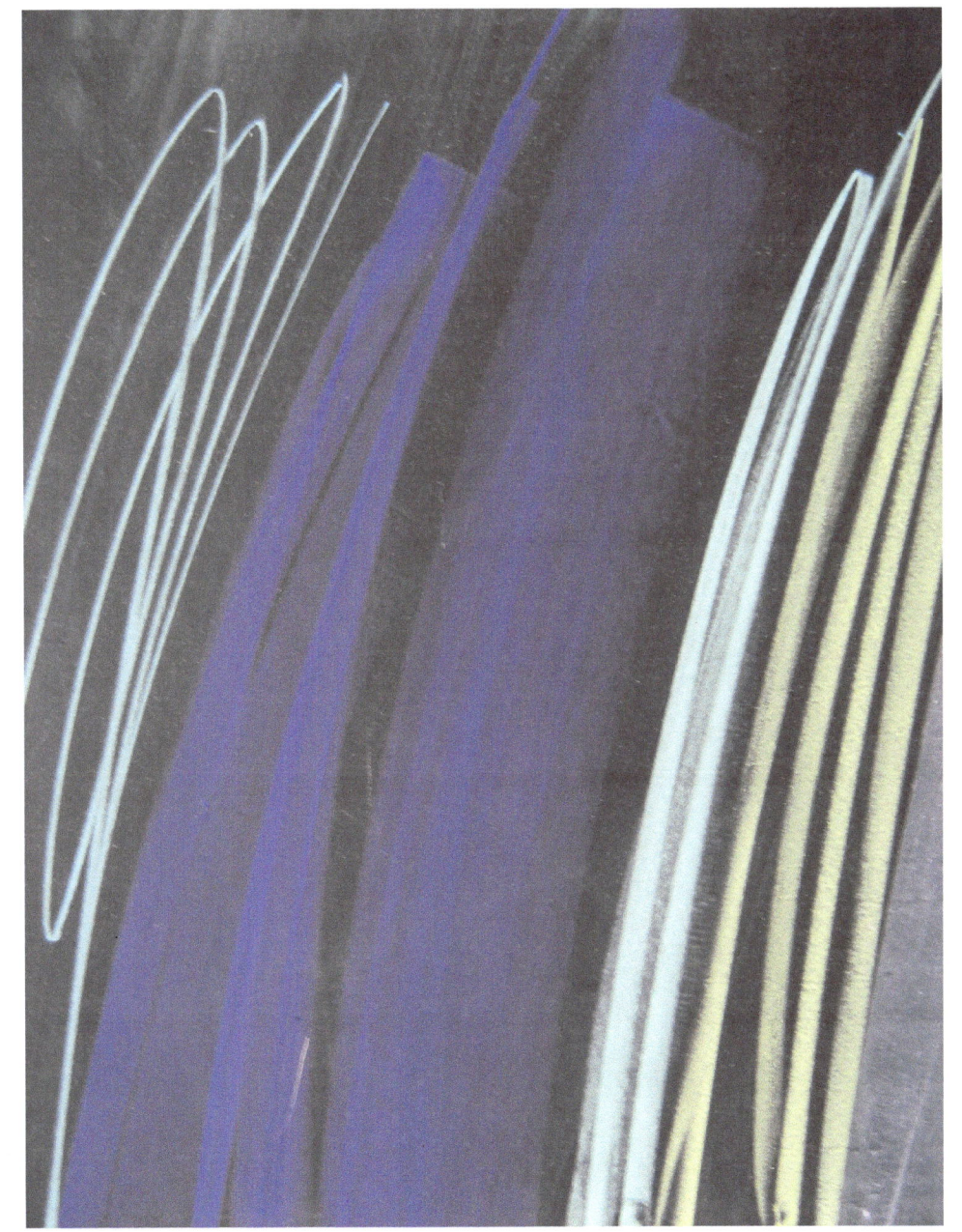

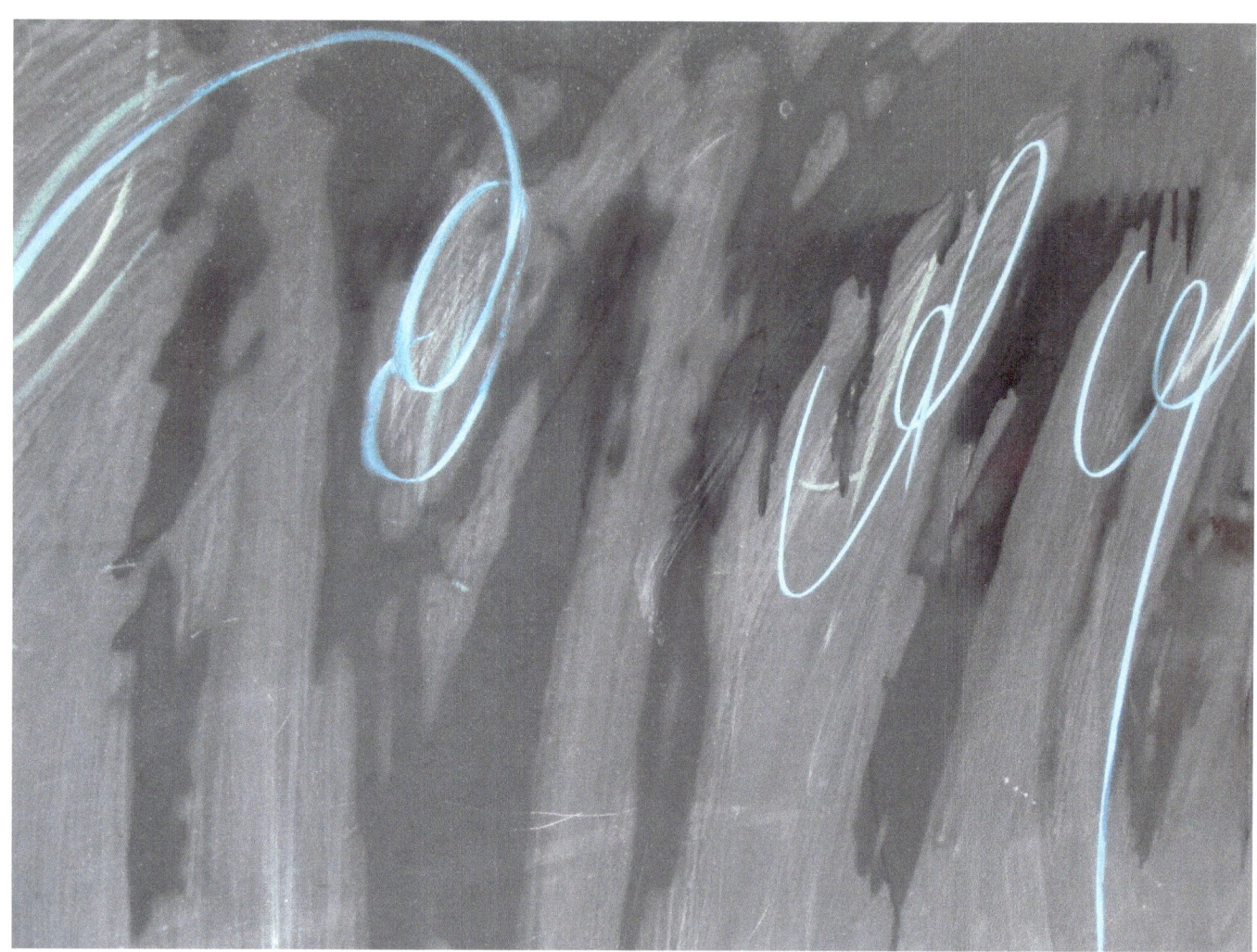

silhouettes catching rain
faces become profiles
where smiles and frowns don't show
the shadows are bound by light

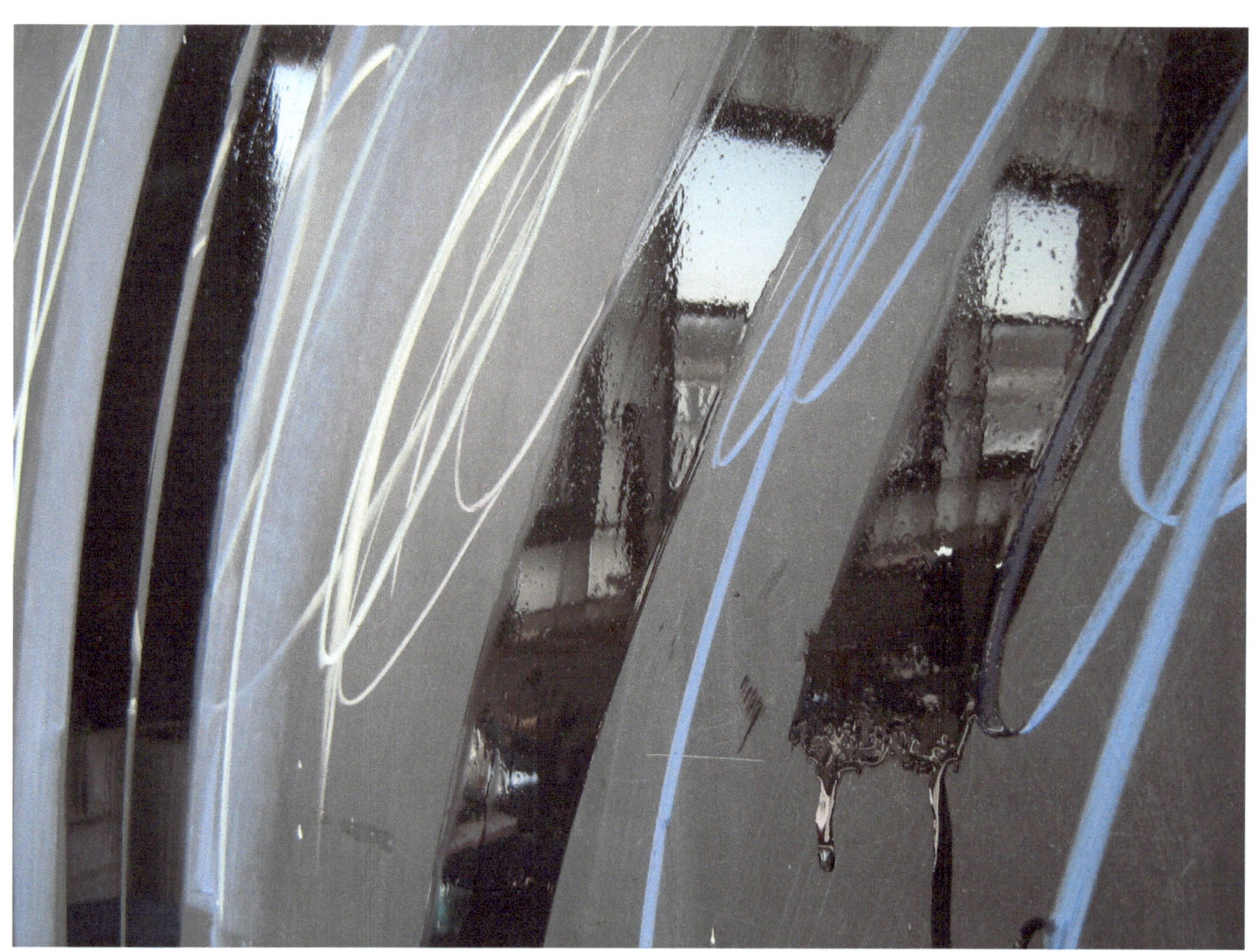

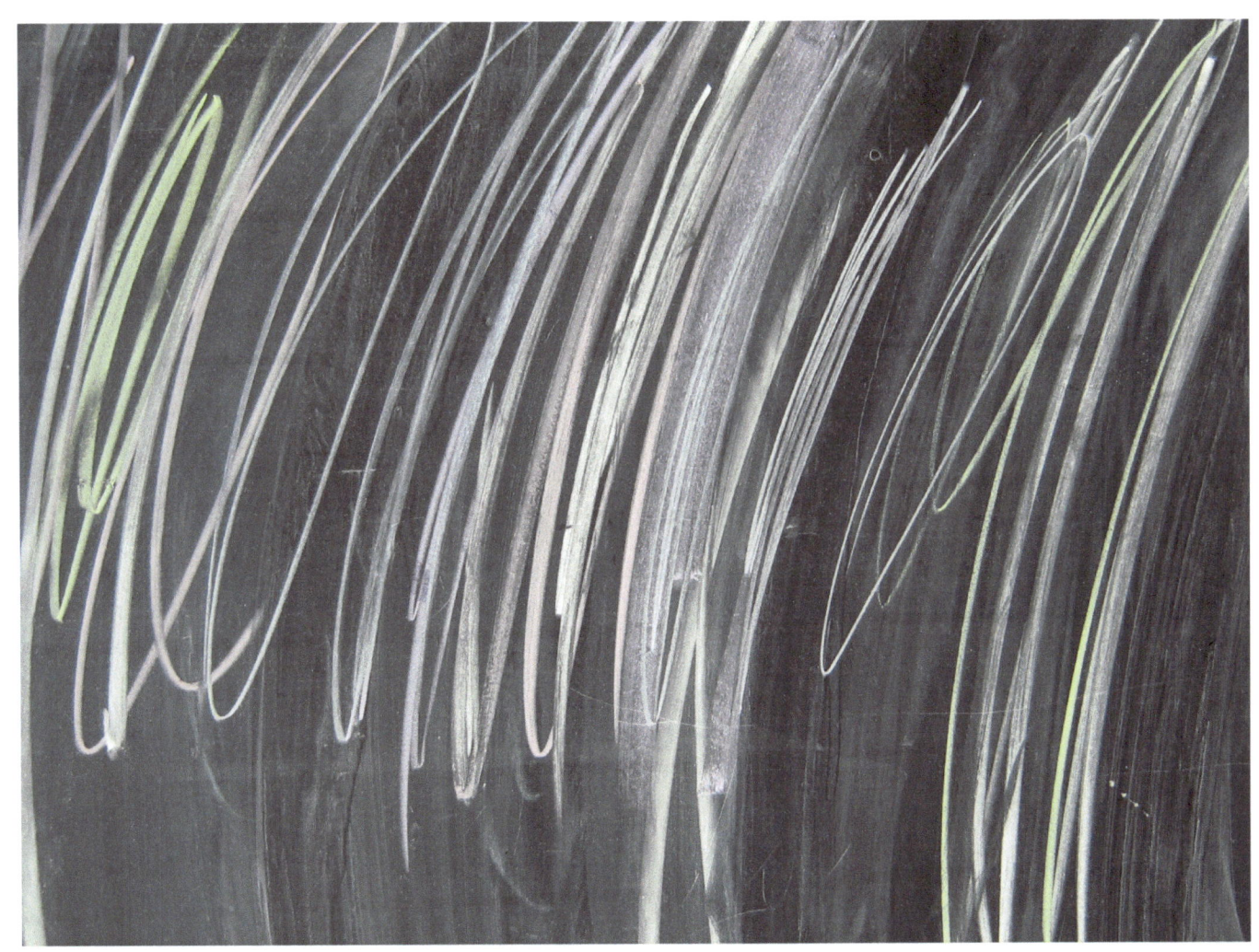

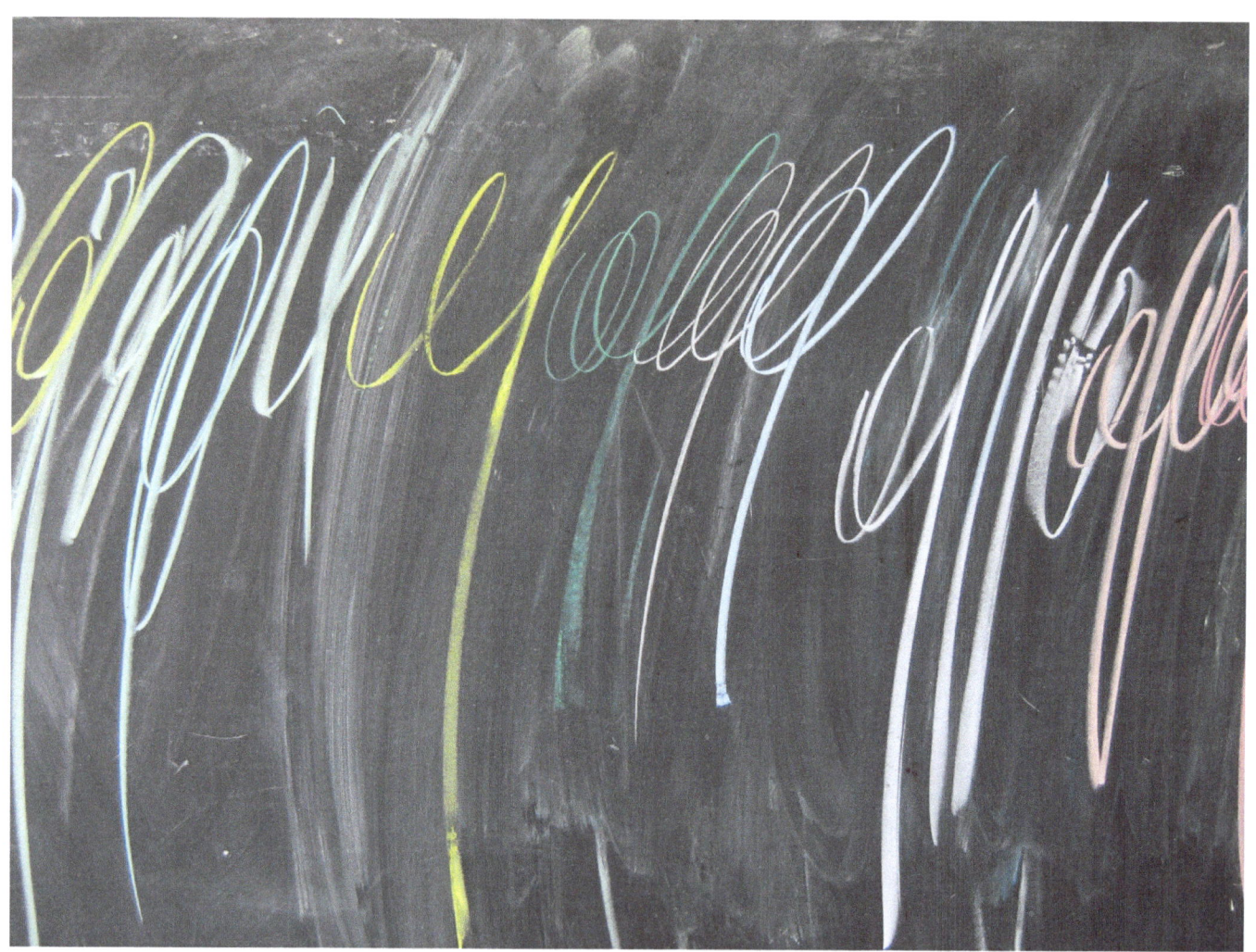

ancient Arabic ritual
yellow storm prays
spirits dance mist
born breath bloom
flowers aroma eye

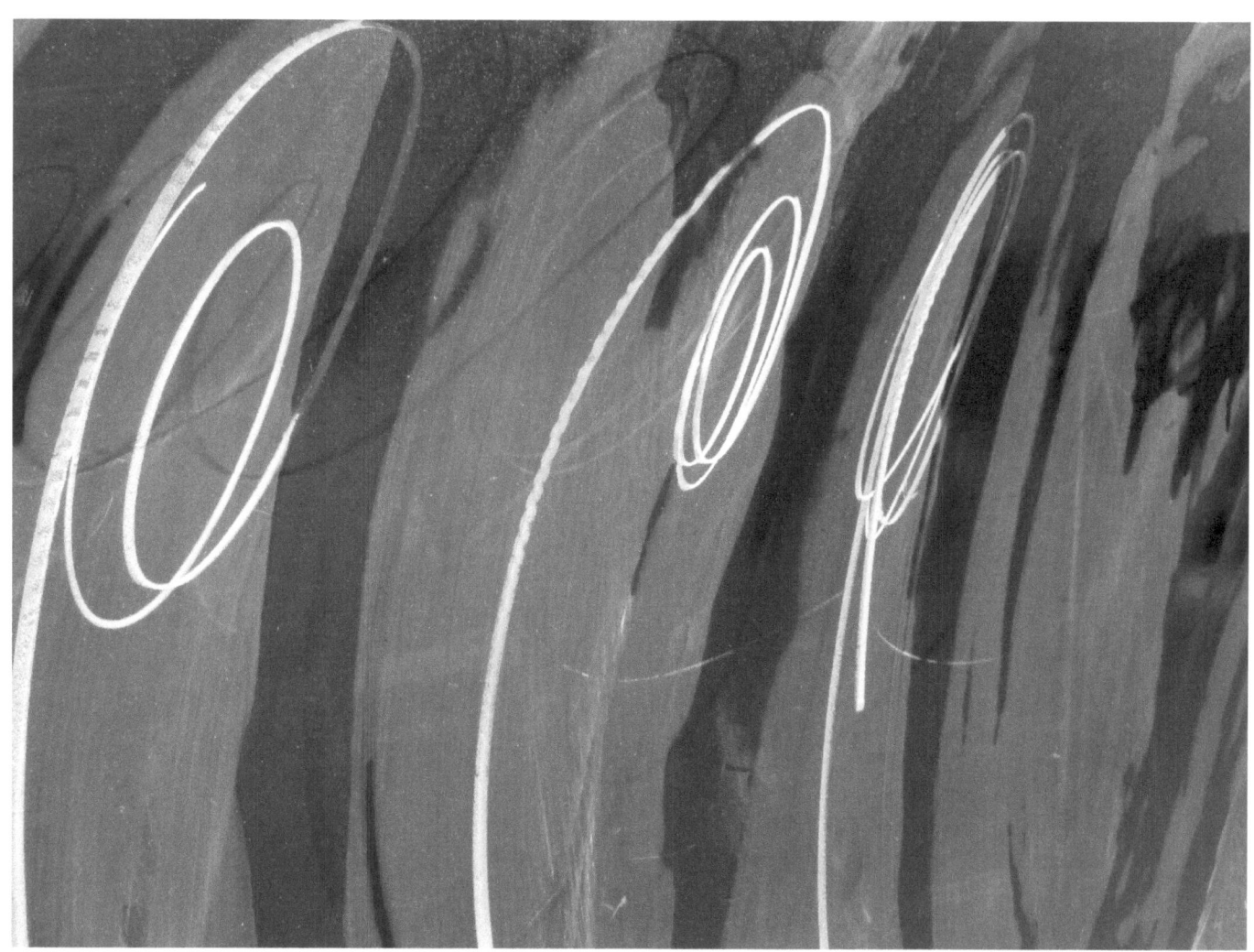

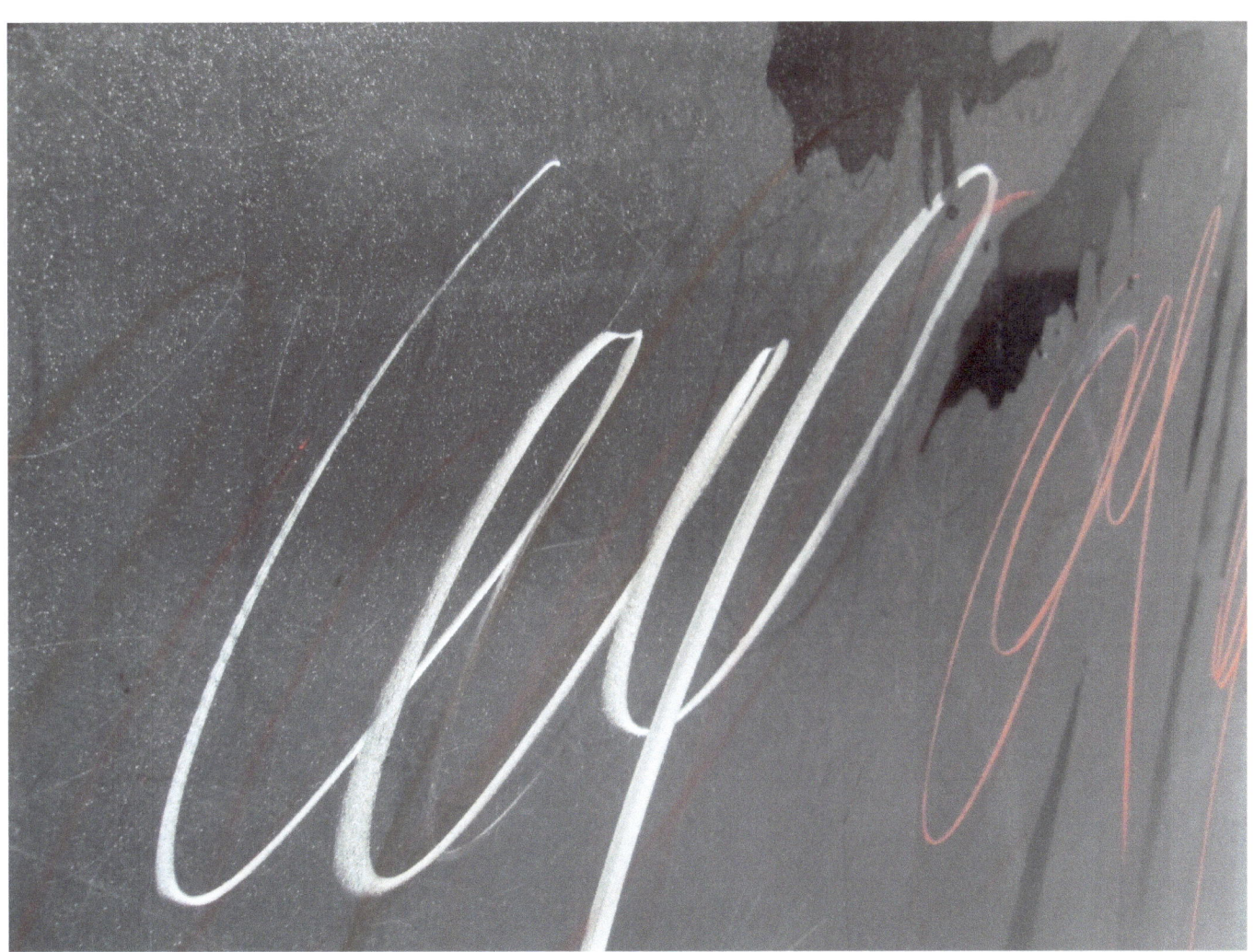

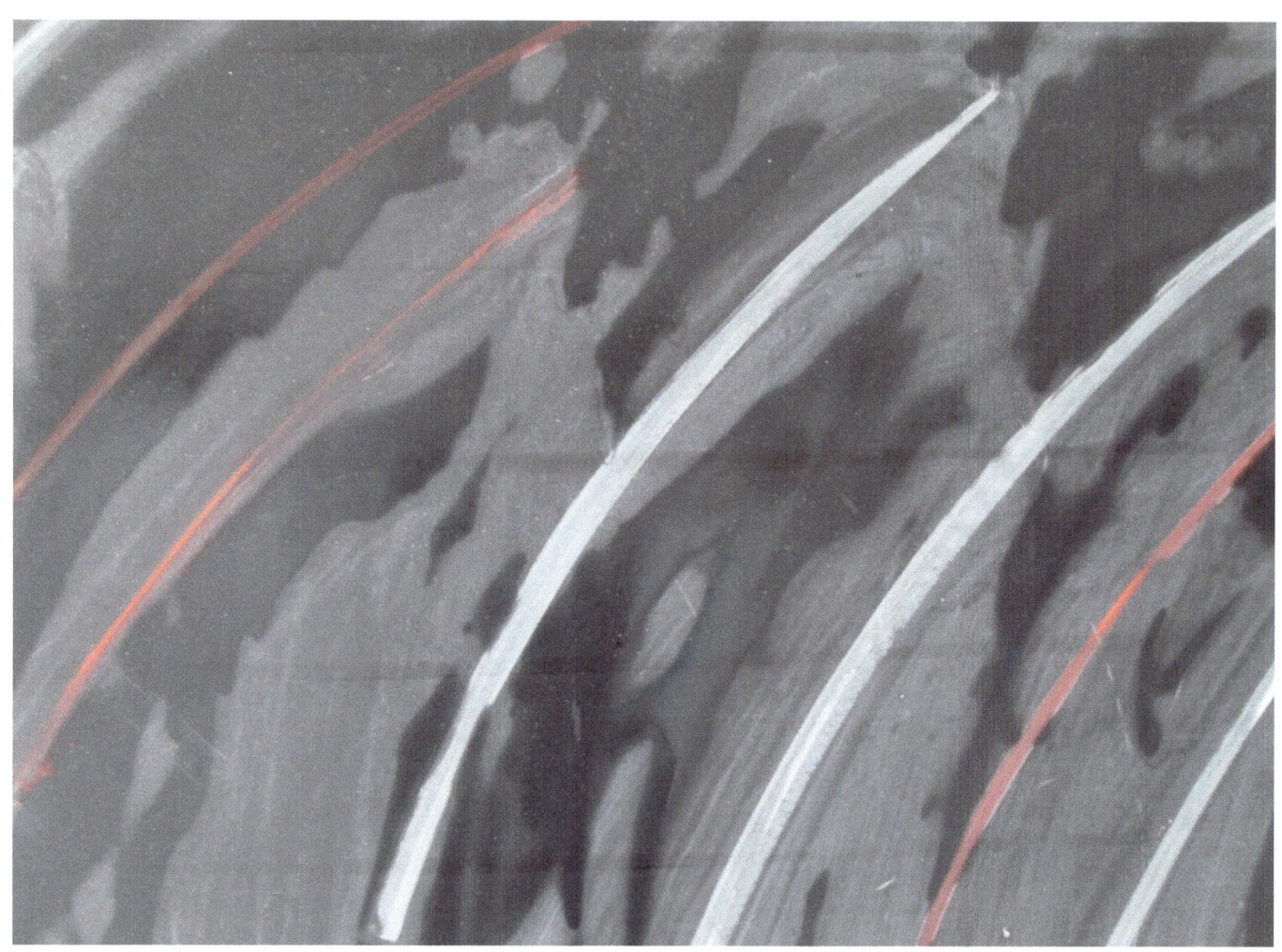

sky paints
ocean sings
earth dances
timeless time
endless ends

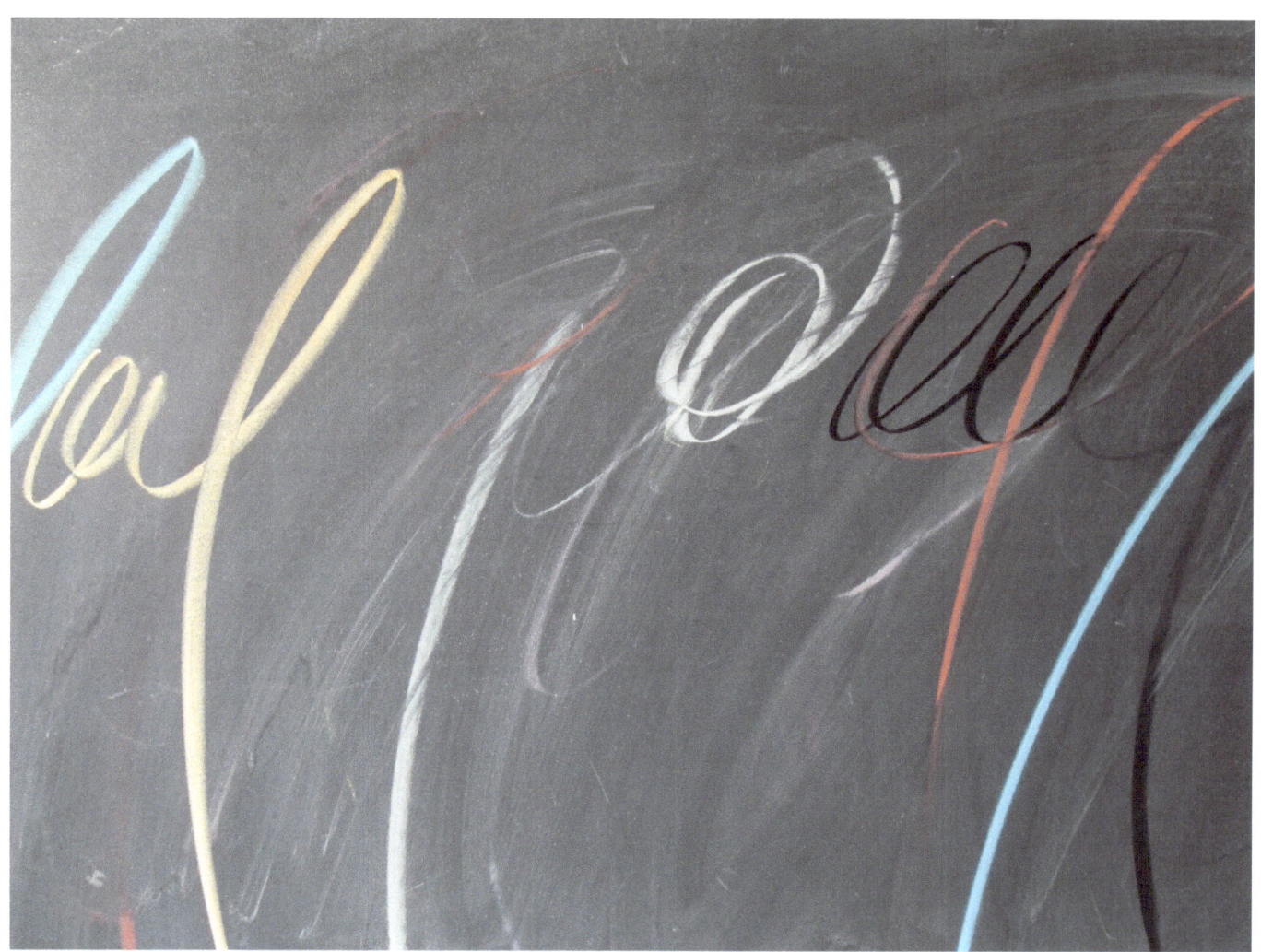

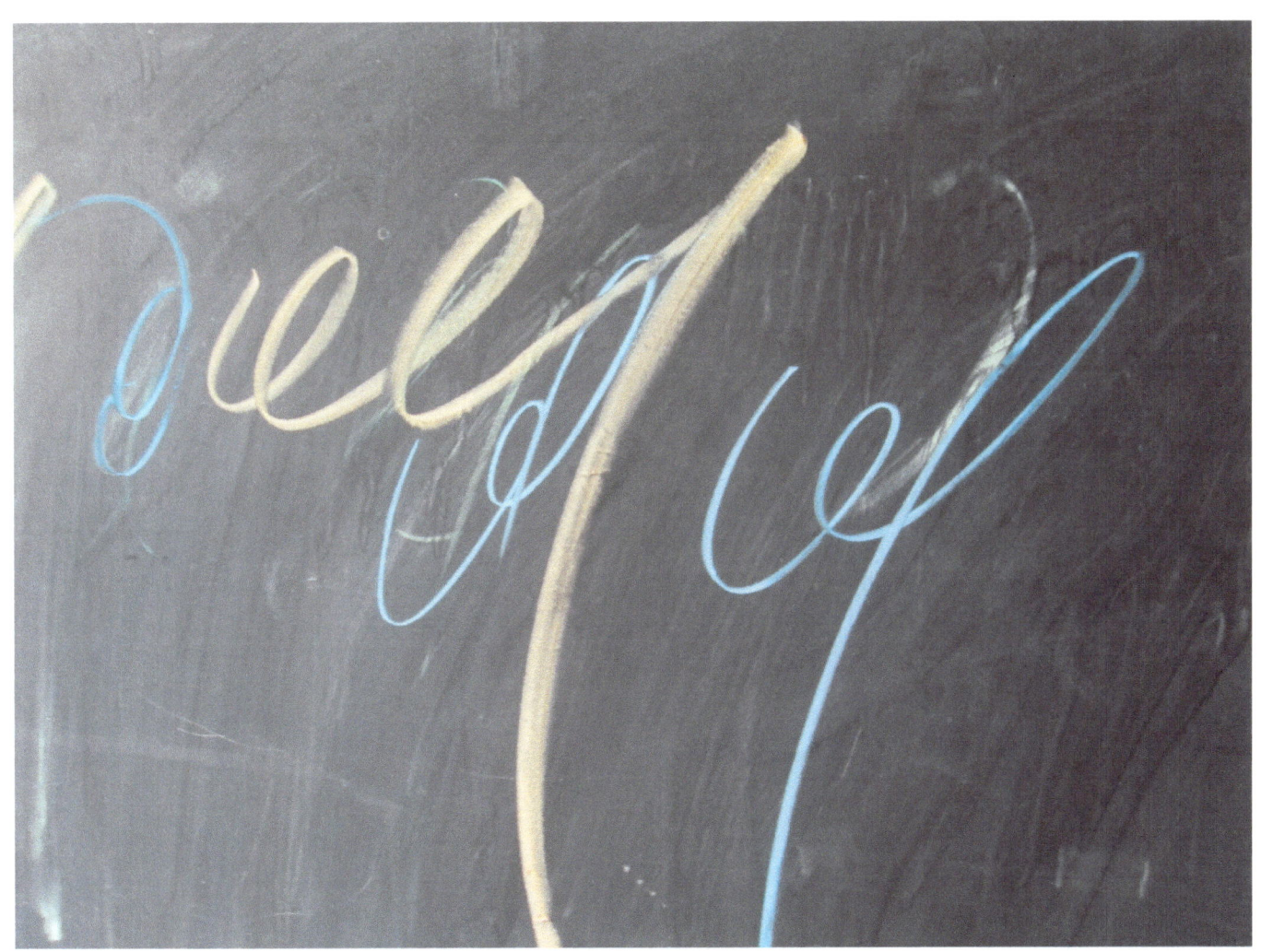

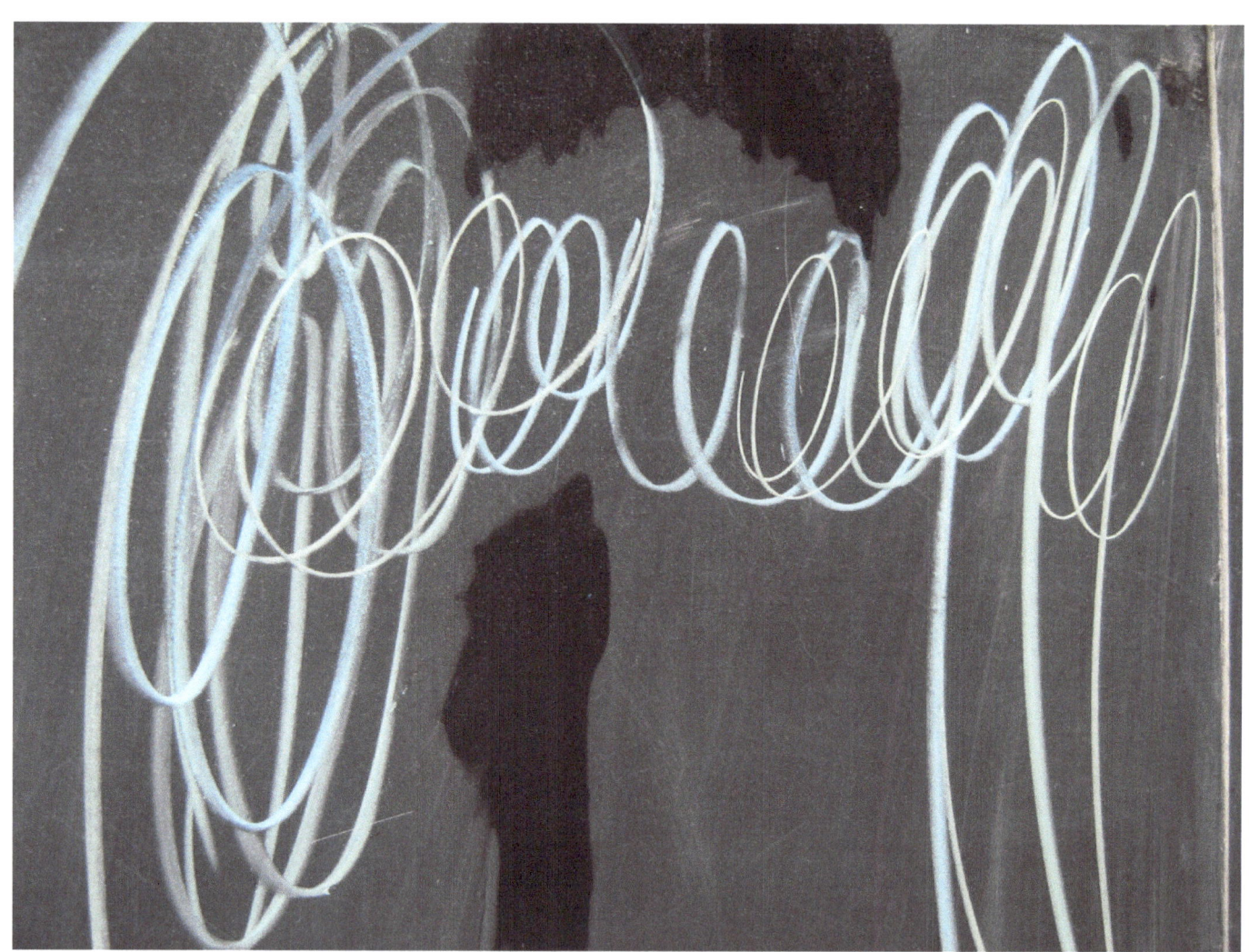

rings sound
pouring lemongrass
a caterpillar walks
ghosts whisper
people speak

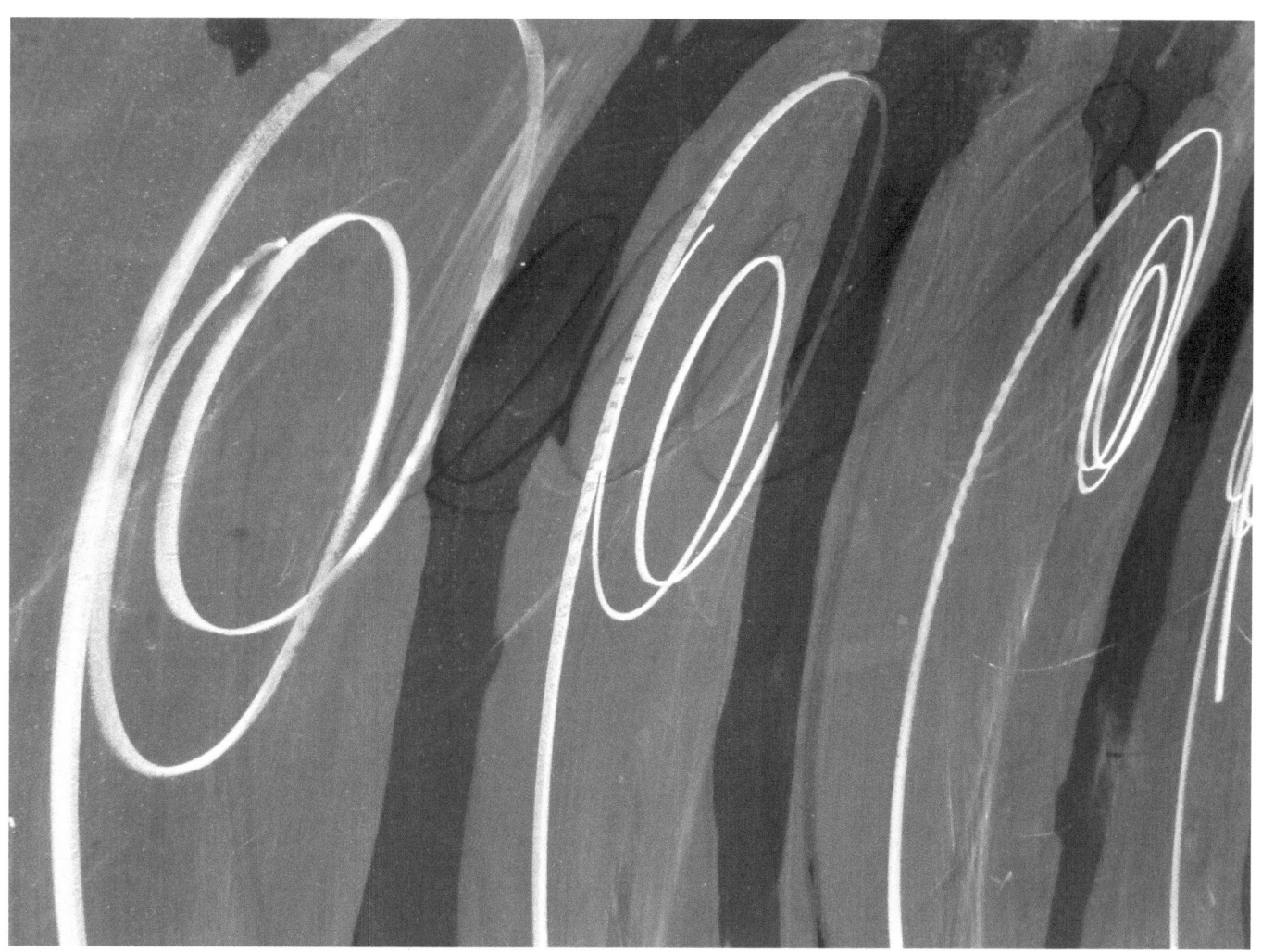

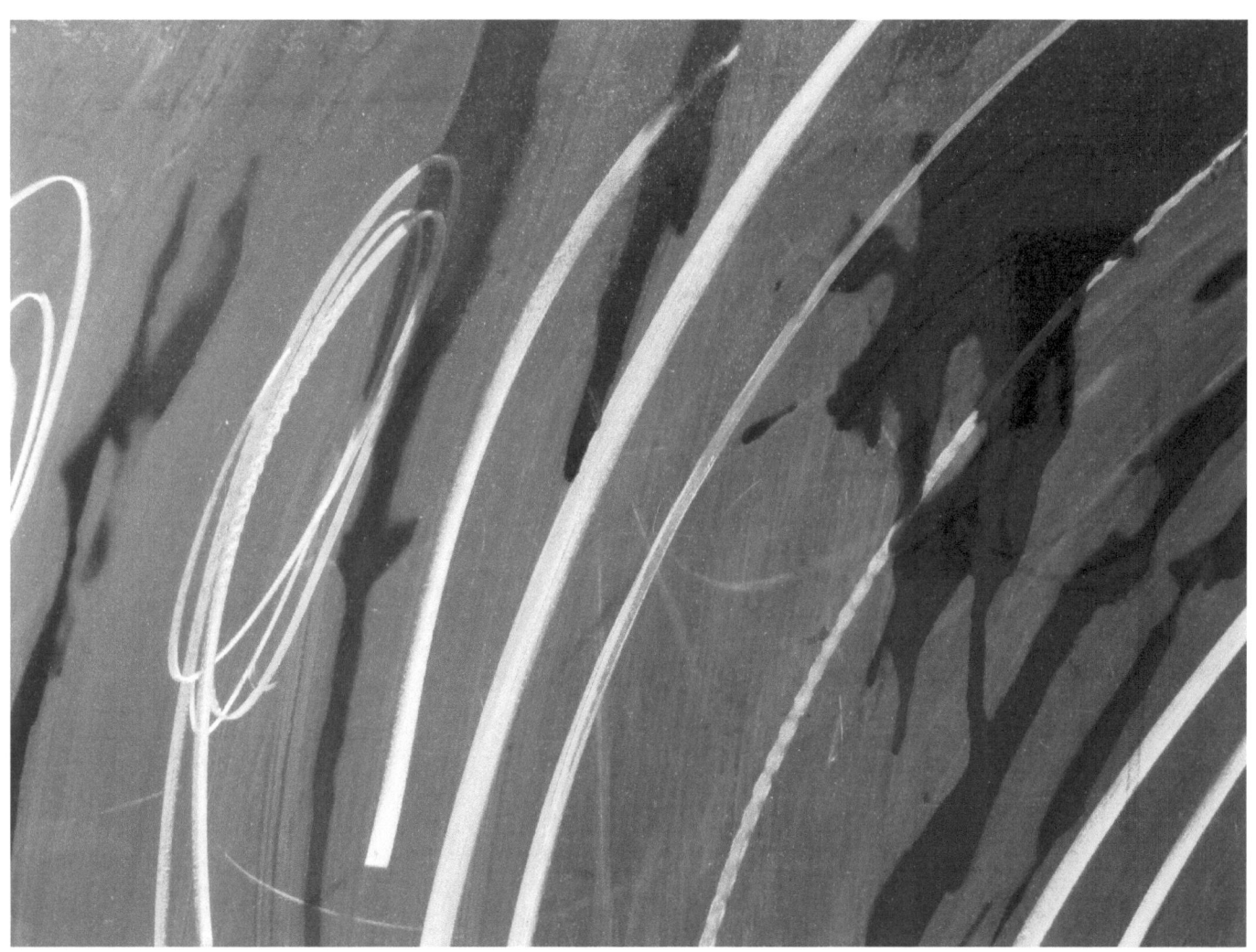

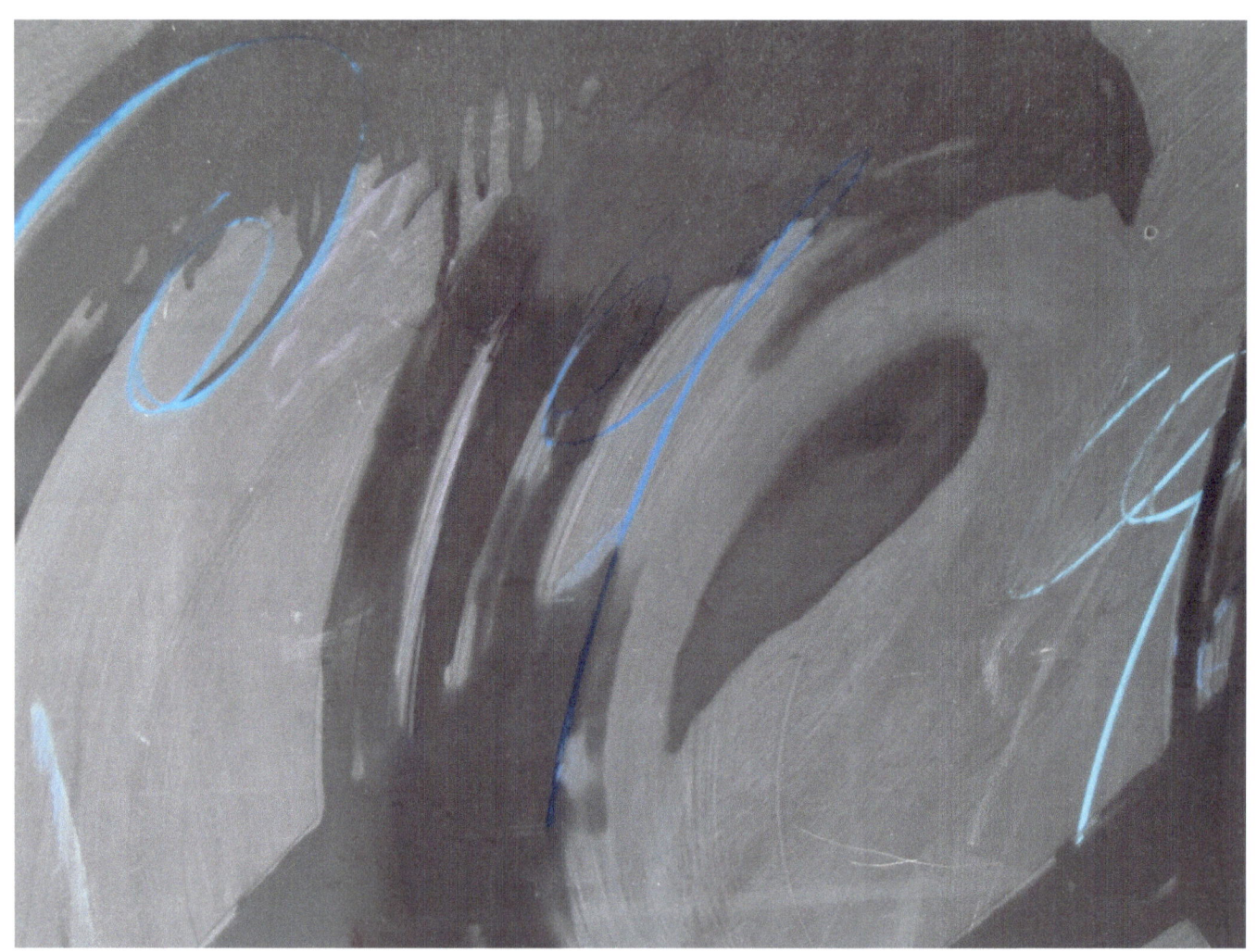

I am the stone
you are the fire
I am the sea
you are the sky
I am the mountain
you are the forest

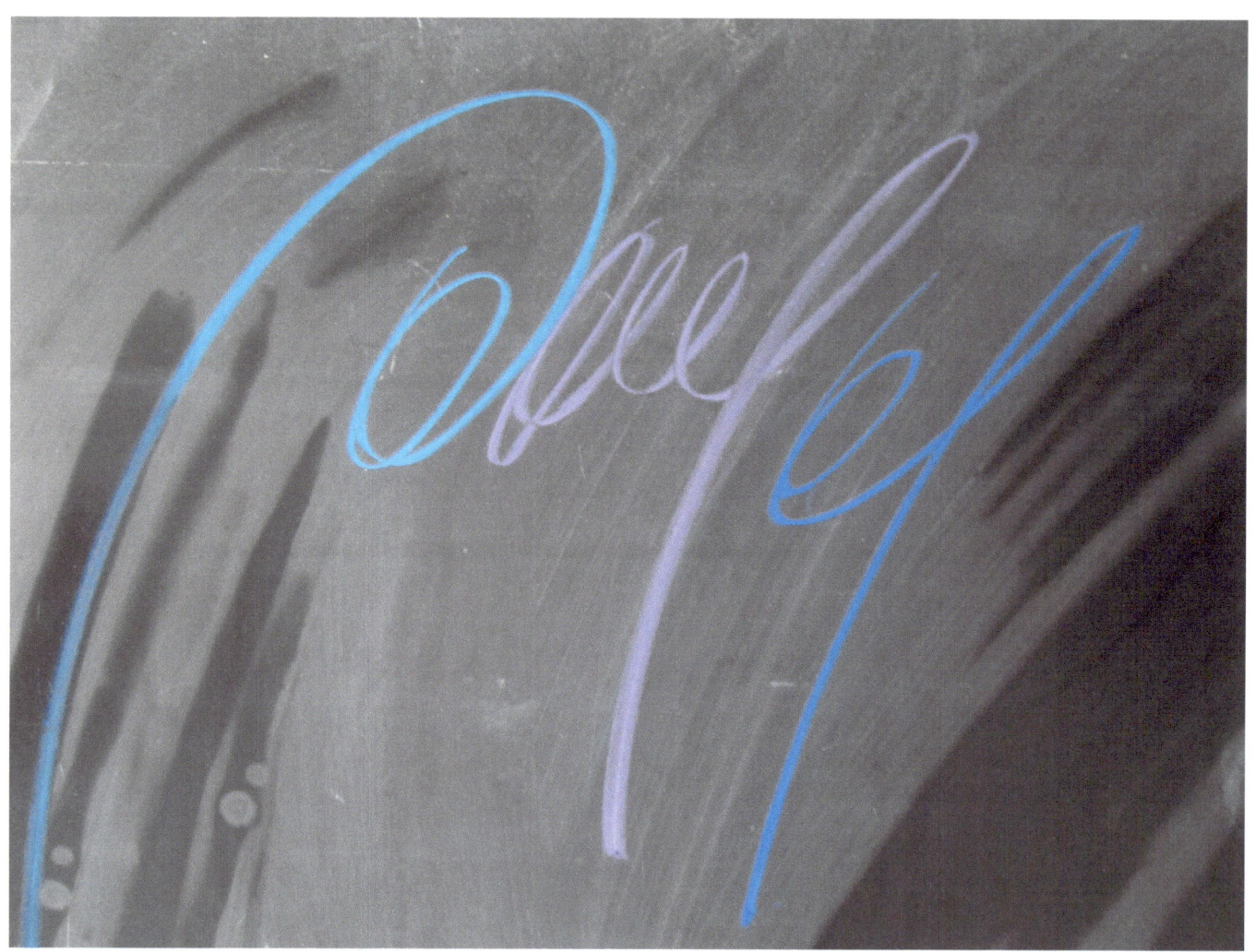

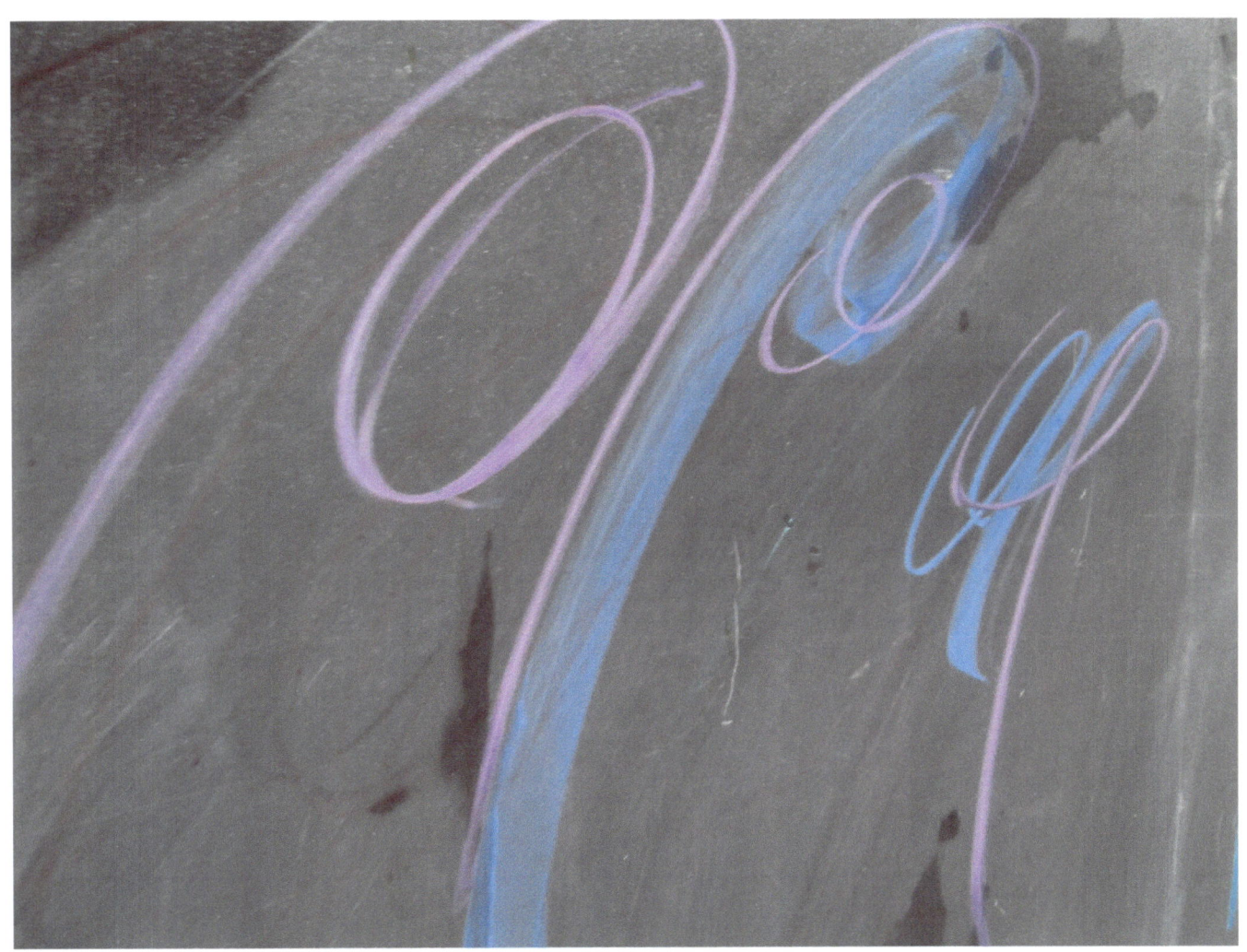

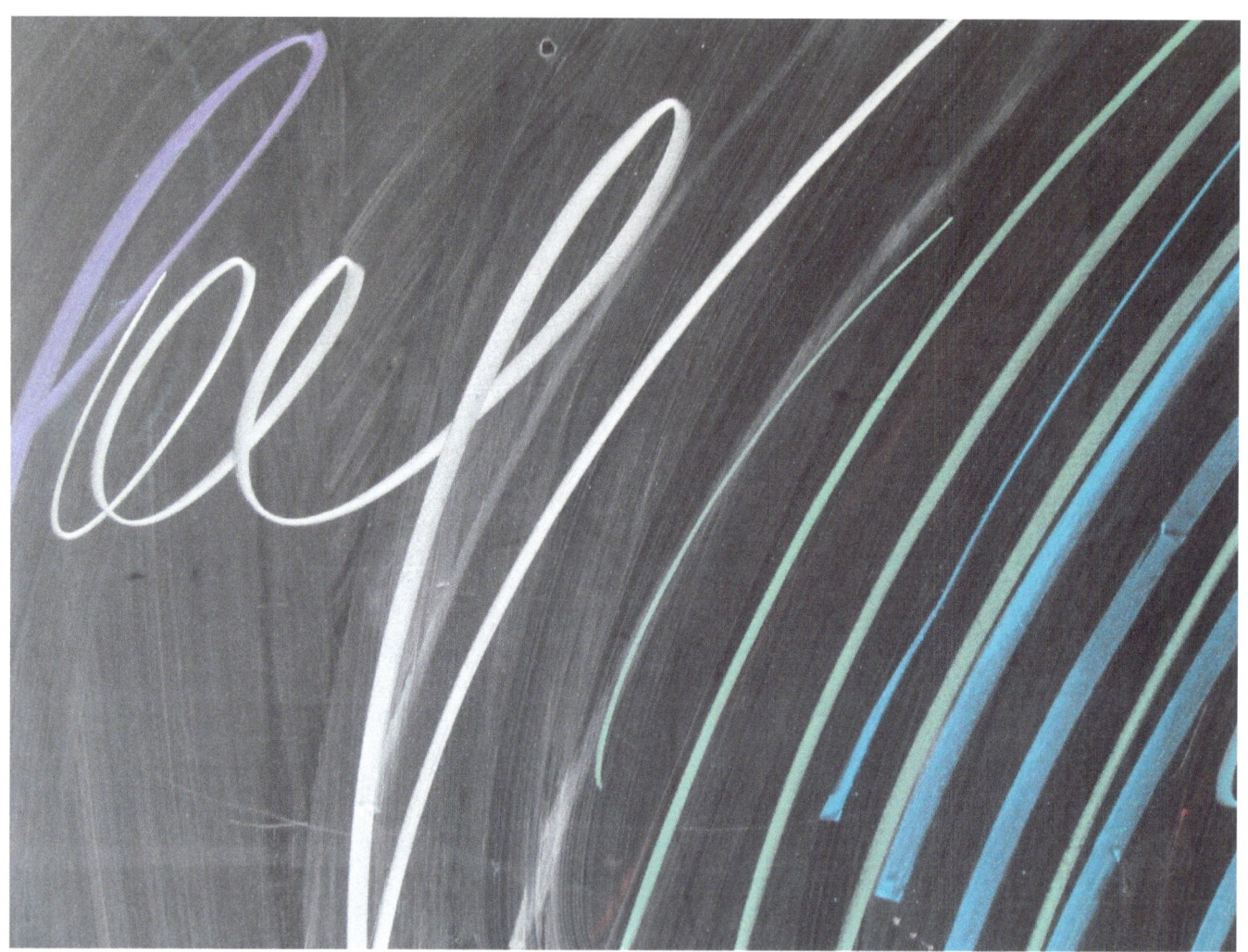

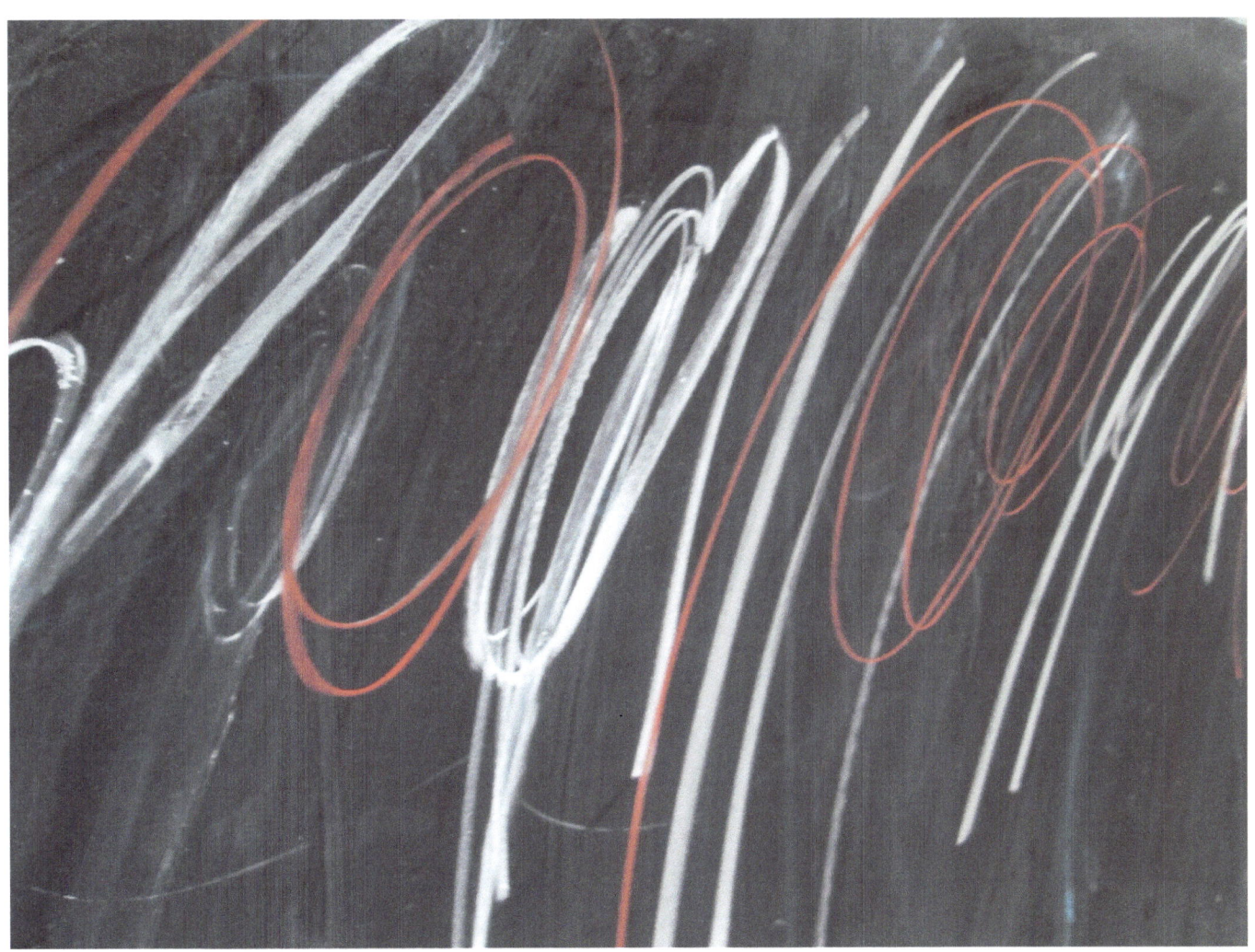

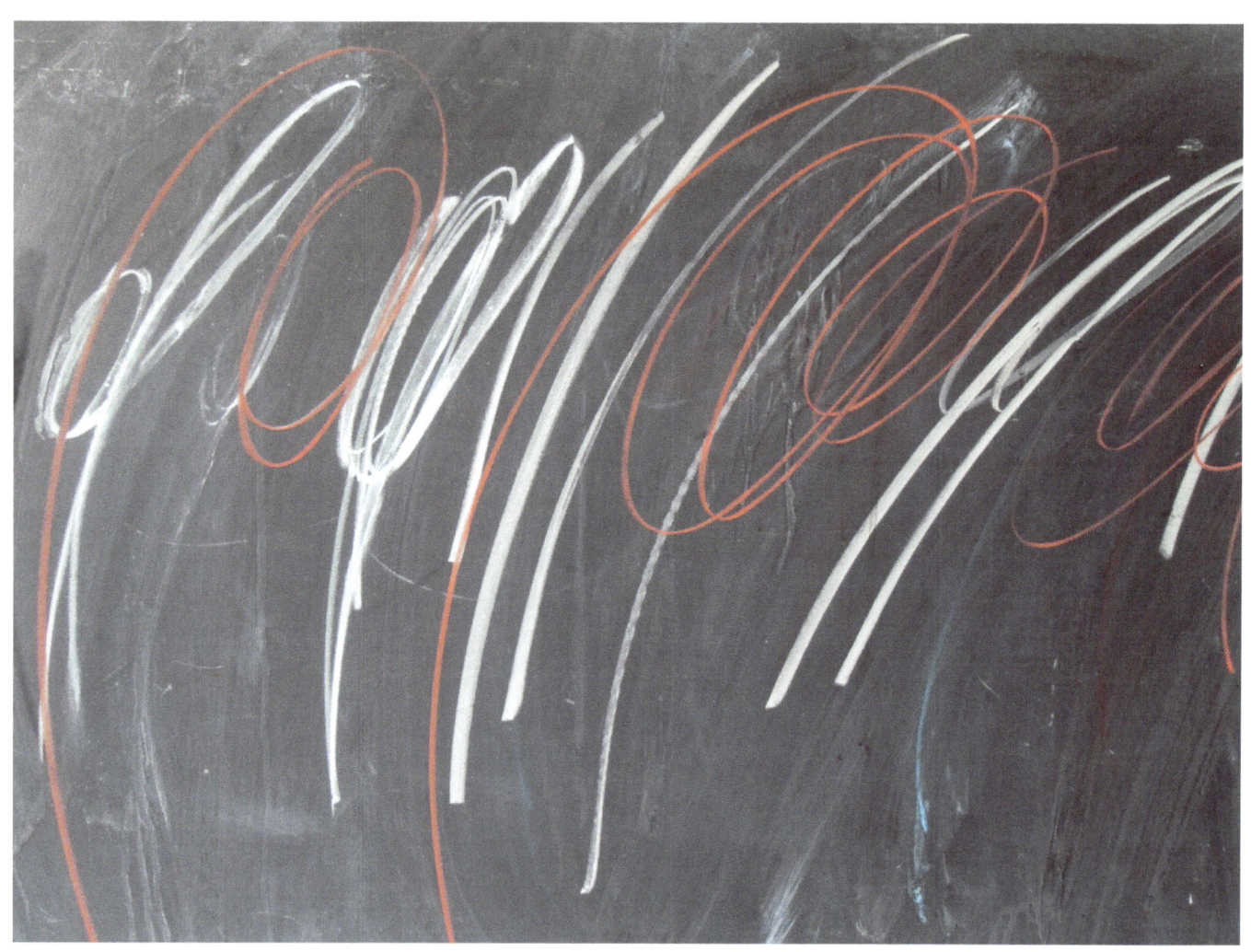

wicked flower
thorns are fresh
their beauty hibernates in winter

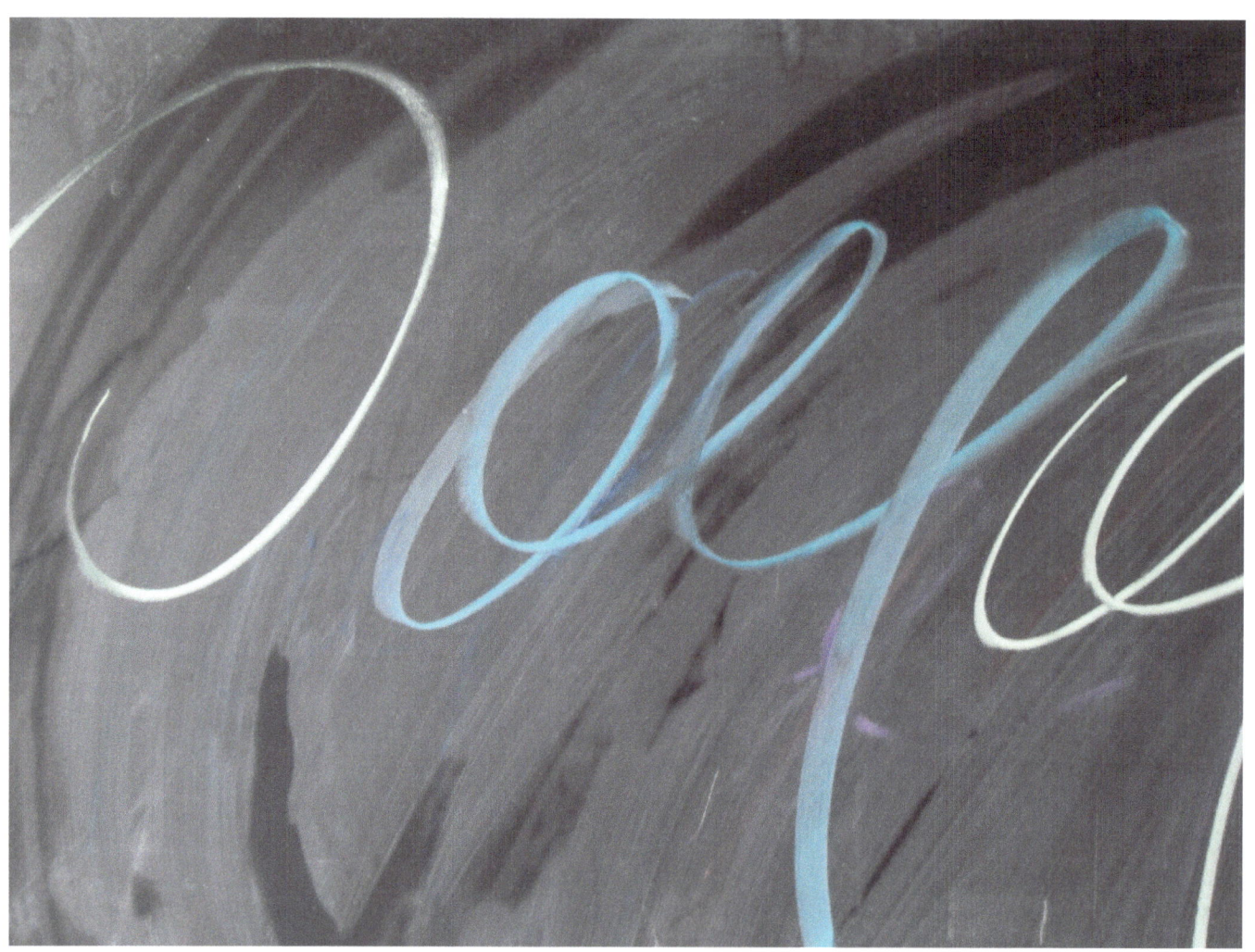

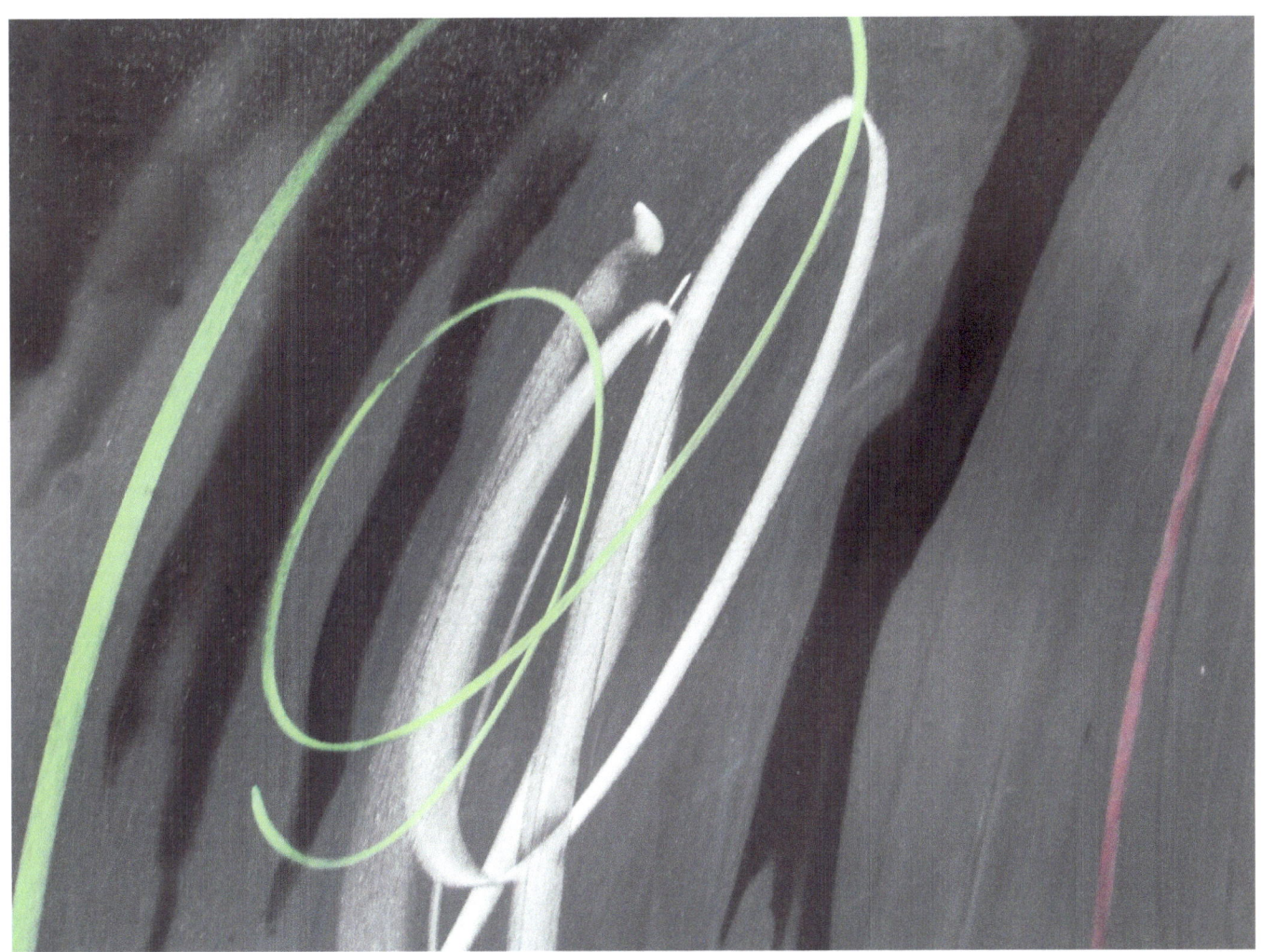

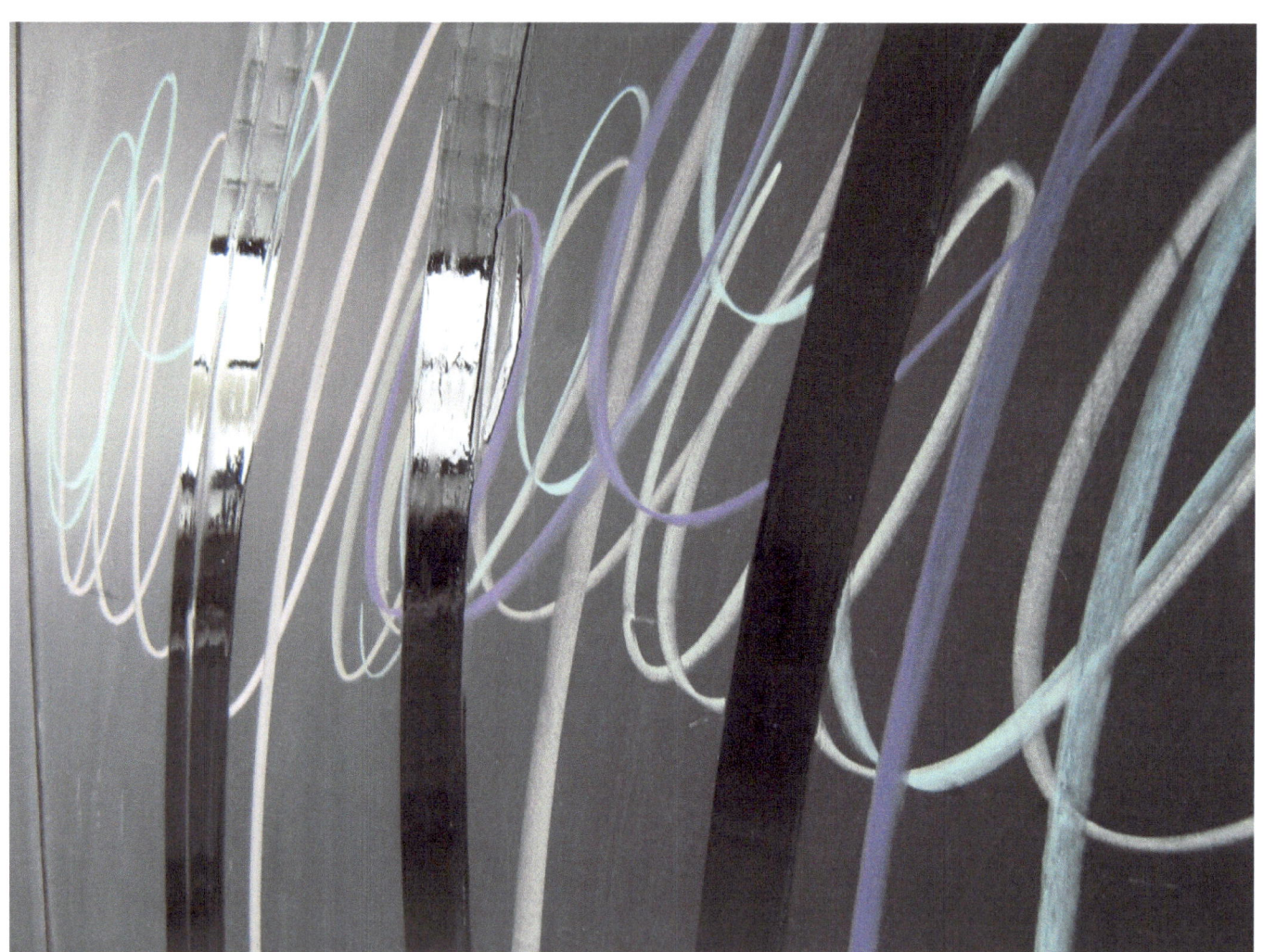

sounds you can't hear
visions you can't see
flavors you can't taste
you are returning home

ABOUT THE AUTHORS

Jack Doehring is a Los Angeles, California based writer and visual artist who graduated from the University of Michigan School of Art & Design. Doehring has exhibited his paintings and drawings in solo and group shows throughout California and in Michigan. Jack Doehring's writing is influenced by world culture and religion. His current visual art focuses on the abstraction of the human figure and objects from everyday life exploring space, color and rhythm.

Sarah Miller's multimedia works have been featured in solo and group exhibitions in museums and galleries, including the Corcoran Gallery of Art and the Phillips Collection, the first museum of modern art. Her work is represented in private collections throughout the United States and in Asia. Public collections include the National Gallery of Art library, Washington, D.C. Sarah Miller has been on faculty of diverse institutions ranging from juvenile detention centers and liberal arts colleges to elite universities where she has instructed art history, art appreciation and studio art including multimedia concept driven courses.

For print inquiries of Sarah Miller's 'Open' series, please visit www.aclew.org